C000227835

HISTORIC
of BELFAST

In association with Belfast City Council

HISTORIC PUBS
of BELFAST

Gary Law

Appletree Press

First published in 2002 by
Appletree Press Ltd
The Old Potato Station
14 Howard Street South
Belfast
BT7 1AP

Tel: (0) 28 90 243074
Fax: (0) 28 90 246756
E-mail: reception@appletree.ie
Web Site: www.appletree.ie

Historic Pubs of Belfast

ISBN 0-86281-833-8

Commissioning & General Editor: Paul Harron
Designer: Wayne Matier

In association with Belfast City Council
www.belfastcity.gov.uk/heritage

Title page illustration: detail of floor mosaic, Hatfield House entrance
Cover illustrations (clockwise from top left): Robinson's clock; tilework, Hatfield House;
bar cabinet, The Blackthorn; etched glass window, The Morning Star; tilework, Crown
Liquor Saloon; barrels, White's Tavern; Bittle's Bar; The Garrick; The Beehive
(Photographic credits on page 95)

CONTENTS

Foreword

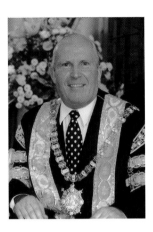

I am delighted to pen the Foreword for *Historic Pubs of Belfast*, a long-overdue compendium celebrating one of Belfast's great traditions, and certainly one of its oldest.

These pages open up a rich, vibrant landscape of gin palaces and snugs, licquor saloons and Temperance hotels, 'wee' bars and super-bars, ladies-only lounges and spit-and-sawdust Belfast pubs that have witnessed some of the most formative – and sometimes tragic – events in the city's history. They unlock a city of distinctive people and landmark buildings, many long since gone. This book also catalogues many of Belfast's modern pubs, forming a continuum that is unlikely ever to end.

Café and bar culture in the capital city of Northern Ireland is thriving. This book offers a chance to reflect on previous eras when Belfast was developing rapidly. During the 18th and 19th centuries, as now, growth in the city's pub-life reflected a boom in its fortunes. Later, when the economy faltered and Belfast and its people experienced conflict, the downturn was reflected in the change and loss of many of the bars that had once seemed like institutions in Belfast's social life.

This book, therefore, is about much more than drinking-houses. It chronicles a unique part of Belfast's heritage. Belfast's pubs are intrinsic to its culture today, and will, no doubt, be central to its future.

The Right Honourable
The Lord Mayor, Councillor Jim Rodgers
March 2002

Introduction

There's an old trick question that still does the rounds of Belfast's bars. A bloke propping up the counter winks at his mates and asks an unsuspecting know-it-all how many pubs were once serving drink along the length of some well-known city street. The know-it-all will mentally progress along the street in question and start counting off the bars on his fingers. Eventually he will arrive at a total, and the questioner will smile knowingly and then tell him he's wrong. The answer – in practically every case – is none.

As the questioner will then point out, almost all the old bars of Belfast were located on street corners and their addresses were not that of the main road, but that of a side street, so it could be easily identified which corner they were on.

And that's the easiest way to single out the city's most historic pubs. If the bar is on a corner, no matter how modern it may appear to be, the chances are that it has been around for quite a while. Of course, it is a rule with exceptions. Pubs that were formerly hotels may not necessarily have been on corners and some of Belfast's oldest pubs are to be found in the middle of narrow alleyways, but generally it's a good rule of thumb for the discerning drinker in search of a watering hole with a past.

In many ways it is remarkable that any of Belfast's old bars have survived at all. Social changes, economic factors, wholesale redevelopment, the 1941 Blitz and the bombing campaign of the 1970s have all played a part in whittling down the city's plethora of pubs. Here's a striking example of how the number of bars has declined. An irate Temperance supporter wrote to the *Belfast News-Letter* in 1900 complaining that 'a man from Queen's Island with wages in his pocket has to pass 67 public houses on his way to the head of the Shankill Road'. How many bars would that route take him past today? Certainly nothing like 67.

There was a time, however, when Belfast had just one pub, but that was when the city wasn't a city; in fact, it wasn't much more than a small collection of houses. Belfast's first recorded inn was called Sir Moses' Cellars, an alehouse named after Moses Hill, a young officer from Devonshire who came to Ireland in 1573 in the service of the Earl of Essex. It was mentioned in a report by the Plantation Commissioners in 1611, which noted that Belfast had 'one inn with very good lodging which is a great comfort to the travellers in these parts'. Some say that the Sir Moses' Cellars was still serving Belfast folk at the beginning of the 19th century.

The steady growth of Belfast's licensed trade in the 1600s was directly proportional to the city's population expansion. As the number of inhabitants topped the 1,000 mark, more taverns joined Sir Moses' Cellars to meet the demands of a thirsty clientele. By 1665 the town fathers were sufficiently alarmed by the increase in drinking establishments and associated boisterous behaviour to decree that 'no inn-holder or ale-seller within the borough shall suffer any person, unless a lodger in his house, to drink or play at any game whatsoever after the hour of nine at night'.

The curfew did little to diminish the popularity of Belfast's alehouses, however. Within a century the population had grown 18-fold and one in every 17 houses was occupied by a licensed publican who dealt in beer and spirits, although most of them supplemented their incomes with other trades. At this time, many of the premises relied on travellers for their business. Passenger and mail coaches usually started and finished their journeys at well-known inns, taverns and hotels and a number of them became official booking offices as well as providing refreshment and accommodation for passengers.

By the time Queen Victoria ascended the throne in 1836, there were 346 tavern keepers in the city. Many of them were concentrated in small areas – in Barrack Street, for example, there were 15 pubs out of a total of 53 places of business. Others were exploring a new source of customers. The railways were beginning to spread out across the land and just as inns had developed a relationship with the coaching industry, so the pubs of the mid-19th century began to foster links with the new train companies. By the middle of the century, however, they were also being seen not just as places for drink, food and a bed, but also as venues for entertainment. Some of the city taverns began to develop into singing saloons, chiefly aimed at the working class, although a few encouraged the gentry as well. The Star Saloon, which opened at 21 Ann Street in the 1850s, was one of the earliest examples of this type of establishment, although some of its competitors were rough, bawdy places with 'disreputable female vocalists who dared to show their brazen and drunken faces before the very lowest audience that could be collected in Belfast'.

It was at this time that snugs began to be a regular feature of pub interiors. In the singing saloons they allowed the upper classes to enjoy the entertainment without having to distastefully mingle with the common folk, or be subjected to their ridicule and insults; while in taverns without entertainment the snugs were ideal places for ladies to seat themselves, since most bars around the city were still very much male dominated and the presence of a woman at the counter would have been regarded with scandalised horror. Indeed, some bars maintained a men-only policy until well into the 20th century – in the 1940s, Kelly's Cellars had a sign denying admission to unaccompanied women while McGlade's Bar in Donegall Street was challenged in the courts over its men-only policy in the public bar as late as 1979.

But in the late 19th and early 20th centuries, women were rarely seen in the spit and sawdust environment of the working man's pub. These bars were often located at the end of a row of terraced houses and would support whole families, who usually lived in rooms above them. The Old Lodge Road, for instance, had 17 of these family pubs at one time. They formed a well-trodden local triangle, the other two points of which consisted of the bookie's and the pawnbroker. Women, if they were permitted in the bar at all, used a snug or a small side bar with its own door, and would have often beaten a path from there to the pawnbroker; while in the main public bar the bookie's runner, who took bets for the customers and collected their winnings, would have had his own reserved seat at the counter.

As the 19th century drew to a close, the extent of public drunkenness began to be a distinct cause for concern for the authorities. There was even a bill laid before Parliament entitled the Drunkards' (Ireland) Bill, though its draconian proposals failed to gain significant support. In 1902, the New Licences (Ireland) Act severely curtailed the number of new drinks licences issued – a move which was welcomed by most publicans, since they feared over-saturation of the market and the increase in irresponsible licensees providing ammunition for the growing temperance movement. From 1893 to 1901, there had been 1,703 new licences approved in Ireland; in 1902 not a single one was granted. Another change came with the Sale to Children Act, which led to the Licensed Grocers and Vintners Association issuing the following notice for members to display on their premises:

SALE TO CHILDREN ACT
WARNING TO ASSISTANTS

It is contrary to the wishes of the Proprietor of this Establishment that any Assistant should sell drink to any child under 14 years of age, except in corked and sealed vessels, and then only in a quantity of not less than a reputed pint.

In the late Victorian period, temperance campaigns had been gradually gaining support as drink proved the ruin of many a household. In 1901 the Catholic Church established the Pioneer Total Abstinence Association, while the Catch-My-Pal movement was founded by a Presbyterian minister in 1910. Four years earlier, Belfast Corporation had issued official posters endorsing temperance, much to the dismay of the city's publicans.

The First World War made the lives of the city's bar owners even more difficult. Distilling was halted altogether and beer brewing was curtailed by two thirds. At the same time, the duty on both was increased to pay for the war effort and the hours of trading were reduced from 16 per day to nine. A scarcity of coal also meant that some pubs closed in the afternoon to conserve fuel stocks.

When the war ended, the temperance question reared its head once again. In the 1920s, the government of the newly created Northern Ireland state came under intense pressure from such groups as the Temperance Council and the Ulster Women's Temperance Association to completely ban the sale of alcohol. The licensed trade was deeply concerned that even if full prohibition was not implemented, some fairly swingeing restrictions might be imposed. At a meeting in a hall in Arthur Street on 9 October 1922, the Belfast and North of Ireland Distillers and Wholesale Wine and Spirit Merchants Association passed a resolution 'protesting emphatically against the offer of the Prime Minister of Northern Ireland to initiate, without public inquiry of any kind, legislation directed against the licensed trade based on the advice of the teetotal party'. The Ulster Vintners Association accused the Prime Minister of a 'breach of faith' and that same month the Ulster Anti-Prohibition Council was set up. The threat of prohibition faded, however, as the lessons of its imposition in the United States became apparent, and ironically the consumption of drink fell sharply during the inter-war years without any significant official interference.

However, that did not stop the anti-drink lobby doing whatever it could to reduce the popularity of Belfast's pubs. In 1936 the tactics of the temperance crusaders prompted the Belfast and Ulster Licensed Vintners Association to make an official complaint to the Royal Ulster Constabulary over 'so-called religious gatherings' outside bars on the Crumlin Road and York Street every Saturday night. 'The noise and din created when they commence to sing and preach is terrific,' said the exasperated society. 'Meetings are invariably held at a corner where there is a public house. The members concerned do not mind a meeting being held there at intervals, but do object to one every Saturday night.'

With the coming of the Second World War, the city's bar owners had more than the occasional religious meeting to occupy their minds. Pubs were issued with strict air raid instructions – if a warning was sounded and the alert continued after 10 pm closing time, the owner of a pub was not compelled to turn his customers out into the street 'but he must obey the licensing laws in every other respect and see that no alcoholic liquor is sold'. Few publicans thought that they would ever have much need to worry about air raids, but then came the Blitz of 4 May 1941, and many historic pubs in the heart of old Belfast were wiped out by the torrent of high explosives that rained down on the city. Bars in High Street, Skipper Street and Church Lane were particularly hard hit by the onslaught, and although some were later rebuilt, others never reopened. Probably the most notable pub casualty of the German bombing was the once-famed Peggy Barclay's Tavern in Sugar House Entry.

In the post-war years, the building boom and the relative prosperity of the 1960s brought many changes to Belfast, and not least to its pubs. Redevelopment and population shifts accounted for many a pub's demise. The clearance of the area around Millfield and Smithfield, for example, spelt the end for many long-standing bars, and the decline in the number of people living and working around the docks meant the disappearance of literally dozens of pubs that depended on local communities for business. In the first half of the 20th century, there was a pub on virtually every corner of the Newtownards Road to serve the shipyard workers, but by the 1960s their numbers were dwindling.

Of the bars that were left, many were undergoing a radical transformation. Out went the old wooden counters, hard seats and tiled floors; in came formica benchtops, leatherette and foam seating, carpets and wooden flooring. 'Until quite recently, customers were content with traditional surroundings, but lounges, formica, and fancy lighting have almost ousted the immemorial snugs of Belfast' lamented architectural historian Charles Brett.

Even more immemorial snugs were ousted when the Troubles began to wreak destruction and violence on Belfast. 'Belfast had – until the bombing campaign of the 1970s – a fine collection of Victorian and Edwardian public houses,' wrote historian Jonathan Bardon, but by 1975 more than 200 had been destroyed or badly damaged by bombs. Many people were killed in these attacks, which often came without warning of any kind, and the result was that most city centre bars either closed their doors in the early evening or were largely deserted. During the dark days of 1976, the climate of fear was such that several Belfast pubs put up signs declaring that strangers would not be served. Some bars were never rebuilt after being wrecked by bombs; others simply shut their doors because of the lack of trade.

More changes have been wrought by the dizzying dance of ownership among the licensed trade. Most bars have changed hands frequently during their lifespan. 'There are 1,625 pubs in Northern Ireland,' an official of the Federation of the Retail Licensed Trade said in 1999, 'and they are all up for sale all of the time'.

New owners very often redesigned their premises, and the more owners of a bar there were, the more changes that took place. The growth of multiple ownership has brought theme bars, high technology fun bars, cool palaces of glass and steel, and retro-fitted spirit grocers. As the industry adapts to meet the demands of its customers, the traditional family-run corner bar is an increasingly rare sight in 21st-century Belfast.

While a good many of the most historic bars in Belfast are long gone, there are some still serving. All, however, have one thing in common – they were places to which customers felt a special attachment and they had a wider significance beyond being somewhere where one simply went for a drink. Belfast's pubs have changed enormously, and will continue to change, but in the process of that ongoing transformation, their integral rôle in the social development of the city should not be forgotten. The next time you're in one of the city's older bars, take a good look around you, for the ghosts of Belfast's past are supping quietly in a corner.

Author's Note

The ever-changing nature of the pub industry in Belfast has meant that it has not always been easy to trace the history of a particular bar. Records are few, memories are subjective, addresses change, owners move on, bars are renamed – the result is often a tangle of half-facts, myths and ambiguous details. I've no doubt that a regular or two in some of the city's bars will cast their eyes over these pages and mutter darkly something like: 'He's got his facts all wrong, this bar was opened in 1820, not 1880. And he never mentioned the day the Duke of Wellington shot the top off a bottle of stout from this very bar stool a week before the Battle of Waterloo.' Well, if that's the case, don't keep it to yourself – tell Appletree Press and your opinions may well be included in any future edition of this book. You can write to them at:

The Old Potato Station, 14 Howard Street South, Belfast BT7 1AP, or contribute your thoughts via their website: www.irelandseye.com

This book is not intended as a definitive guide to *all* of Belfast's historic hostelries, rather as an entertaining *selection* of pub descriptions from across the city.

Cross-references to pubs are given in CAPITAL LETTERS.

Key

 The pint glass symbol denotes an establishment which, at the time of going to press, still functions as a public house (although not necessarily trading under the same name given in the heading).

HISTORIC PUBS
of BELFAST
A–Z

THE A1 BAR | 36 Waring Street

Wherever there are journalists, it's a dead certainty that there's a pub not too far away, and with the *News Letter* and *Northern Whig* offices just a stone's throw from the A1 Bar, it's hardly surprising that it became a favoured haunt of scribes in search of a sup. But Benny Conlon's bar was not just a place where reporters, photographers and compositors and printers swapped yarns and did their socialising. It also served as the unofficial strike headquarters for at least two disputes involving newspapermen and their owners. And in addition to all the newspaper folk, the A1 was also a popular rendezvous for a variety of post office workers, solicitors, dockers, sailors and civil servants.

With a pedigree dating back to around 1870, one of the A1 Bar's most endearing features was its apparent lack of a single level interior surface – the counter, shelves, walls and floors all sloped erratically – and its air of authenticity meant that it often provided the backdrop to television dramas about the Troubles. Noteworthy adornments included original gas light fittings and a sliding door for the gents' toilet, which was apparently rescued from a tram. Sadly the redevelopers' wrecking ball spelt the end for this colourful watering hole at the end of the 20th century, although at the time of writing a portable building housing a bar nostalgically named 'The Press Box' stands on the site of the A1.

THE ABERCORN | 7–11 Castle Lane

The most colourful proprietor of licensed premises on this site was a Miss Eliza Johnston, who in 1868 named her hostelry the Abercorn Arms and Ulster Gridiron. Before that, it had been Adam Black's Hotel in the late 1840s and then Phillips' Hotel, but it was Miss Eliza Johnston who really put The Abercorn on the map.

'Eliza was a striking personality,' wrote historian Alfred S. Moore in his book, *Old Belfast*. 'Six feet tall, wearing invariably red bandana headgear, a long gold chain, wide sleeves and a multi-flounced skirt, and always with a bunch of keys jangling. Her hands were enormous and never went direct to their aim when they grasped anything, but minced about, feeling for it.'

Renowned for her generosity, Eliza proved such a popular hostess that the Lord Mayor and leading citizens of Belfast made her a special presentation when she retired from the Abercorn in 1881. Eliza's successor in the early 1890s was a Mrs Litchfield from Manchester, who ran the Abercorn Hotel and Restaurant until 1916, apart from a brief interlude when a Miss Winter was the owner.

In 1916, The Abercorn was acquired by Charles Thompson. The premises continued to be popular but found its true niche in the 1960s and 1970s as a city centre entertainment venue, hosting local entertainers and top cross-channel acts in its 400-seater lounge. The blackest day in The Abercorn's history came on 4 March 1972, when a no-warning terrorist bomb exploded in the packed premises on a Saturday afternoon, killing two people and injuring more than 130 others. The premises did reopen following the tragedy, but they never regained their previous level of popularity and closed some years later.

THE AMERICAN BAR | *65 Dock Street*

Some say that The American Bar is so called because it was near here that the first US troops landed in Belfast during the Second World War. It's true that the GIs stepped ashore not far away – at Dufferin Quay on 26 January 1942 – but that isn't the reason for this pub's name, for records clearly show the American Bar to be much older than that.

We need to go back another hundred years to find the first instance of a dockside pub with a flavour of Uncle Sam. In the 1840s, a woman called Ellinor Charters ran the American Hotel at Princes Dock, a cul-de-sac which connects with Dock Street. By the 1860s, the premises were known as Samuel Savage's American Hotel and within another ten years the American Inn was established nearby on the corner of Dock Street and Short Street. The bar has remained at this location ever since.

A gathering outside The American Bar in the 1930s (Hogg Collection, Ulster Museum)

Just to confuse things, the American Inn was rechristened the American Hotel in the 1890s under the ownership of a spirit dealer called H. Cusin. Just before the turn of the century, it was taken over by H. Bell and by 1910, Patrick Crealy, who was probably a relative of John Crealy, the proprietor of the nearby ROTTERDAM BAR, was in charge of the hotel. Hugh Kelly took over from Patrick Crealy in 1931 and within five years he had dropped the word 'hotel' altogether and the premises became known simply as 'The American Bar'.

So how did the pub really get its name? One likely suggestion is that it relates to the large number of people who boarded emigration ships sailing from Belfast to America in the years following the Great Famine of 1845–50 – which was just about the time Ellinor Charters was establishing her American Hotel in Princes Dock. Certainly by the time the GIs stepped off their troopships almost a century later, the welcoming sight of the American Bar was already firmly established in Belfast's dockland.

THE BEATEN DOCKET | *48–52 Great Victoria Street*

The modern pub that stands on this site dates from 1985; but had you been strolling down the relatively undeveloped Great Victoria Street in the middle of the last century, you could have called in for a glass or two at the Downshire Arms Hotel and Refreshment Rooms that once stood on this spot.

John Bains' hotel was the end building in a trio of hotels that are still in existence as licensed premises today. In 1856, when the Downshire opened its doors, the CROWN LIQUOR SALOON on the opposite corner of Amelia Street was known as O'Hanlon's Ulster Railway Hotel and ROBINSON'S next door was called the Dublin and Armagh Hotel. All three of them owed their existence to the lucrative trade brought to the city by the railway terminus across the road. There was even room for a fourth establishment, Miss Rogan's Temperance Hotel, which was slotted between the Dublin and Armagh and Ulster Railway Hotels for a 50-year period beginning in the early 20th century.

Around the time Miss Rogan was setting up in business, the Downshire Arms changed its name to the Adelphi Hotel. The owners were the Flanigan family who had purchased the Ulster Railway Hotel in the 1880s, christened it the Crown Hotel and reinvented it as a temple of opulent Victoriana. In the 1930s, both the Crown and the Adelphi were sold by the Flanigans to Patrick McGeeney, who also owned bars at 44 Donegall Quay, which later became the LIVERPOOL BAR, and 22 Dock Street, later to become PAT'S BAR.

Some years later the Adelphi became the Hamill Hotel when it was purchased by the Hamill family, whose most illustrious son, Belfast Celtic player Mickey Hamill, ran the CENTRE HALF BAR off the Falls Road. It was during the Hamill's ownership that the transition from hotel to bar took place – by 1972, the premises were referred to as the Adelphi Bar.

When the Diver family bought the bar from the Hamills and created The Beaten Docket, the upstairs bar was christened the Hamill Lounge as a tribute to its former owners.

THE BEEHIVE | *193 Falls Road*

Unlikely as it may seem, there is a story that the founder of the Scout movement, Lord Robert Baden-Powell, was a regular customer in this distinctive hostelry. It's said that he used to ride down to the bar from a nearby military barracks and enter the premises still on horseback, from where he would order his drink, down it and depart without ever leaving the saddle.

True or not, who can say? What is certain, however, is that the Beehive itself was at one time a military barracks, and for a time also served as a hotel. Figures sculpted in the façade reveal that the bar dates from 1888 and a decorative beehive is also visible on the exterior. The rather eccentric choice of name and exterior decoration is attributed to the bar's first owner – an anonymous

The upper storeys of the former Beehive pub, with its distinctive beehive detail

Dutchman who was an enthusiastic beekeeper and maintained hives in the garden of the premises. The theme was continued inside where a copper panel was decorated with a beehive motif, and there was also an array of attractive tiles depicting scenes from Shakespeare's plays and the changing seasons.

Severely bomb-damaged during the Troubles, the Beehive has been replaced by Caffrey's and Oísíns Bars, although a large portion of the original façade remains visible today.

BITTLE'S BAR | 103 Victoria Street

The often haphazard layout of Belfast's streets meant that some oddly shaped buildings were constructed to fill the cramped city centre spaces created by the

The 'smoothing iron'-shaped corner of Bittle's Bar

interlocking web of roads and laneways. The narrow triangular structure of Abercorn Buildings, constructed in 1868, was by no means unusual, nor was it surprising to find a bar occupying its most acute angle. These pubs became known throughout the city as 'smoothing iron' bars because the shape of the building resembled a household clothes iron.

It took some time for Abercorn Buildings to be occupied – two years after their construction all four stories still lay empty – but by 1892 McCarthy's Dolphin Bar was installed at No 103, and the Abercorn Rooms for public meetings were created at No 101. Interestingly, next door to the Dolphin Bar, at No 105, was the Victoria Bar, run by Thomas Conlan, who also owned THE KITCHEN BAR in nearby Victoria Square.

Agnes McCarthy, who was perhaps the widow of the original owner of the Dolphin Bar, was the proprietor in 1910, but by 1922 she had sold the premises to two partners called Harrison and Duffy.

At some point many years later, the pub ceased to be known as the Dolphin and became The Shakespeare Bar. A pub of the same name was owned by the Keaveney family and was originally located not far away in William Street South on the site of what is now Littlewood's store.

The Shakespeare sat next door to another pub, the Rose and Crown, and many of its customers were drawn from the theatrical business, since the famous Empire Music Hall was just around the corner and the Theatre Royal was not far away in Arthur Street. Jimmy Keaveney, who later ran THE DUKE OF YORK in Commercial Court for more than 30 years, began his lifelong involvement with the bar trade at the Shakespeare, which was owned by his mother.

Jimmy served up his first pint at the Shakespeare in September 1932 and he recalled in an interview many years later that one of the bar's most unusual features was a theatrical insurance scheme known as the Music Hall Artistes' Railway Association. 'These theatre people had their own sort of insurance scheme long before insurance schemes were common,' he said. 'They each paid six pence a week. If any one of them died when they were on tour, they would be coffined and sent home. And the next of kin would get £100.'

The Keaveneys moved on to the Duke of York in 1938 and it appears that the Shakespeare relocated in Abercorn Buildings some time after the Second World War. Two of the ground floor windows in the bar's new home featured portraits of the Bard, and a representation of Shakespeare's head was sculpted prominently on an exterior wall. Many of the interior decorations of the present Bittle's Bar continue the literary theme established in its Shakespeare days.

THE BLACKTHORN | *3 Skipper Street*

A map of Belfast drawn in 1660 names only five streets in the town – High Street, Bridge Street, North Street, Waring Street and Skipper's Lane, now known as Skipper Street. In the centuries since that time, this old city thoroughfare has seen its fair share of pubs come and go. These have included bars like Charles Downey's Hotel and Chop House, a once popular Victorian eaterie that is no longer even a

Behind the bar at The Blackthorn

memory, or Diamond's pub at No 13, which dated from the beginning of the 20th century and was bombed out of existence in the Blitz of 1941. The Blackthorn, although a fairly recent addition, carries on the long line of unfussy traditional bars that have buzzed with conversation and quenched a few thirsts down through the years. Built on the site of the former premises of J. Grant, cork and bottle merchant, the bar was opened as the Albert Inn in 1959 and changed its name to The Blackthorn in the late 1980s.

THE BLOUSE | *54 North Street*

This unusual bar, run by the Ulster Wine Company since the 1930s but no longer in existence, earned its popular nickname because it was one of the very few houses in Ireland in the 1960s and early 1970s to have a ladies-only lounge. The tradition of the Blouse Club was that a man was only allowed into the place if he was accompanied by a lady, and indeed if he was invited by her. If he was alone, the alternative was to go to the Red Hand bar, with its distinctive red decor, old the-atre prints and wooden partitions, or he could have a drink at a third bar on the premises, notable for its portrait of the once-popular music hall entertainer Willie John Ashcroft. He certainly wouldn't have been admitted to the Blouse Club on a Tuesday night, for this was strictly a 'ladies only' entertainment night – though one suspects the designation had a slightly more genteel connotation in the 1970s than it has today.

The land on which the Blouse Club stood may have been one of the earliest grants of land in the city of Belfast, being given to George Theaker in 1619 for a rent of £1 16s 11d 'and two fat hens or capons'. The well-known Belfast firm of wine and spirit importers John McKibbin and Sons had their premises here in 1892, before moving to 7 Waring Street around the turn of the century. For a time, 54 North Street was also the address of the Dockers' Club. Needless to say, however, nobody at that time ever made the mistake of referring to it as the Blouse Club.

THE BODEGA | *4 Callender Street*

With its Spanish name – a *bodega* is a cellar or shop selling wine – and Iberian-influenced decor it might seem that this city centre bar and restaurant is more of an early example of a theme pub than a historic inn, but in fact the Bodega's vintage is much older than its latest incarnation would suggest.

Callender Street derives its name from callendering, which was a process employed in the linen industry. The White Linen Hall, which stood on the site of Belfast City Hall until the end of the 19th century, was just around the corner, but that appears to have been the street's only connection with Ulster's best-known industry. Its links with strong drink and its consumption are much more pronounced, however. For example, the founder of Belfast's most famous whiskey distillery, John Dunville, began production in Callender Street in the early 1800s, and the Bodega was a pub for well over a century before the addition of its Spanish trappings.

It is said that old stables were located here before the first watering hole to be built on the site, the Fox Tavern, opened its doors in the mid-19th century. The tavern was run by a Mrs E. Carmichael in the 1890s and then by a G. Maguire in 1910. In the 1920s, under the ownership of John Cunningham, the premises incorporated the Red Bank bar and restaurant and became a busy lunchtime eating spot.

On the night of 4 May 1941, after the centre of Belfast suffered massive destruction in a German bombing raid, looters broke into the damaged bar just hours after the all-clear was given and not only stole all the drink on the premises but even unscrewed fixtures from the bar counter.

The Callender Street bar adopted its Spanish influence in 1966 when it was extensively refurbished and renamed 'The Bodega'. A tiled roof was installed above the downstairs bar, while the upstairs split-level bar was shaped like a horseshoe. A popular city centre eating establishment, the Bodega survived yet more bombing – this time during the Troubles in 1974 – and continues to be Belfast's little bit of Spain today.

THE BOREEN | *12–14 Church Lane*

Measuring just 22 feet long by 7 feet wide, this tiny bar is reputed to have been the smallest public house in Belfast. It has been claimed that customers were squeezing in here as early as 1840, but this would appear to be contradicted by records from 1850, which show that 12 and 14 Church Lane were occupied by William Fox, haberdasher, and Arthur Anderson, tailor. In 1910, the address was occupied by the Cash China Stores; and even as late as 1936, it was the location of a gents' outfitters rather than a pub.

Many buildings in Church Lane suffered severe damage as a result of the German bombing raid on the night of 4 May 1941. In 1943, the site of 12–14 Church Lane was described as vacant in the *Belfast Street Directory*. The location's connection with the drinks trade seems to date from 1947 when a spirit merchant called Mrs Maguire set up in business there. From 1953 until 1965, the little bar was owned by John Byrne and in the 1970s the owners were two partners called McKenna and McGinley. The Boreen was renamed the Glass Jar just a few years ago, but the petite pub was demolished in 2001.

THE BOTANIC INN | *23–27 Malone Road*

Probably since its earliest days as a coaching inn, students and lecturers from near-by Queen's University have been drawn to this popular watering hole. One of the more notable customers was an Australian Zoology lecturer called Theodore Flynn, who could literally nip across the road from the University's Department of Zoology and Botany for a quick drink or two in the Botanic Inn. Never heard of him? Well, what about his son, Errol, famous for his swashbuckling roles in such movies as *The Adventures of Robin Hood* and *The Sea Hawk*? And Errol's dad wasn't the only celebrity to have propped up the counter of this south Belfast bar. Blair Mayne, the Newtownards-born soldier who was decorated many times over during the Second

'The Bot' – a popular student haunt

World War, was another. And then there was the world heavyweight boxing champion Joe Louis.

Dating from around the middle of the last century, the Botanic Inn has been in the Mooney family since 1919 and has been the cornerstone of an expanding network of city pubs and nightspots that includes MCHUGH'S in Queen's Square and THE NORTHERN WHIG in Bridge Street. 'The Bot', as it is affectionately called, has been restyled on a number of occasions and remains as popular with students today as it was with Errol Flynn's father.

BOYNE BRIDGE TAVERN | *4 Sandy Row*

At one time there were two Boyne Taverns on Sandy Row. The Boyne Bridge Tavern at No 4 was the first to be established, opening its doors in the late 19th century, but when another bar called the Boyne Tavern was opened at the corner of Moore's Place around 1914, locals began to refer to the two pubs as the 'Big Boyne' and the 'Wee Boyne'.

It has been claimed that the Big Boyne's first owner was a Mrs Elizabeth Williams in 1870, although others say that Joseph English, who also ran two other bars in nearby Hope Street and Linfield Street, founded the bar in 1895. By 1907, English had sold both the Boyne Bridge Tavern and his Hope Street Bar to W. J. Turtle, who in turn passed the two bars on to Kennedy Leacock – a colourful figure who was often dubbed the 'Lord Mayor of Sandy Row'. Leacock, who also owned a bar in Pine Street, was the proprietor of the Sandy Row pub for over 50 years. The interior of the Boyne Bridge Tavern was particularly noted for its fine engraved glass windows and its picture of Sir John McNeill's original lattice bridge over the River Boyne at Drogheda.

CAPSTAN BAR | *10 Ann Street*

In the early 1840s, a radical young Belfast journalist named Charles Gavan Duffy was busily turning out a politically explosive newspaper called *The Vindicator* three times a week from his offices at 10 Ann Street. The strident tone of Duffy's articles soon brought him into contact with other leading nationalists of the time, including Young Irelander Thomas Davis, with whom Duffy founded *The Vindicator's* successor, *The Nation*, and John Mitchel, the Dungiven-born lawyer and journalist who ran a series of short-lived nationalist newspapers and published his famous *Jail Journal* in America in 1848.

The strident tone of the editorials issuing from Duffy's Ann Street offices soon led him into conflict with the authorities and on four occasions he was arrested and put on trial for sedition. After he narrowly escaped the death penalty in one trial, Duffy decided that Ireland was too hot for him and he emigrated to Australia. Like many emigrants, he prospered in the New World and within 15 years had become Premier of Victoria.

While Duffy was building a new life for himself in Australia, *The Vindicator's* former offices did not lie idle. Ann Street was then, as now, a busy commercial street. In addition to its many shops, the street was also home to around 630 residents in the 1850s, so there were plenty of potential customers for a tavern. After a few years as a spirit dealers, *The Vindicator* offices became James Young's Circus Hotel in 1860. The hotel prospered for around 20 years before becoming Swanton's Bar, a popular watering hole with the theatrical profession. The existing building at the Crown Entry corner, and presumably the present name, the Capstan Bar, date from around 1905. A copper hood over the doorway bears the embossed image of a capstan while a sign overhead attests to the bar's 1860 origins.

Charles Gavan Duffy, meanwhile, rose to such eminence in Australia that he was knighted and some time later returned to his native Belfast, no longer the dangerous radical but now the respected statesman, Sir Gavan Duffy. Whether or not he stopped off in James Young's Circus Hotel to drink a toast to his past times in *The Vindicator*, we shall probably never know.

CAULFIELD'S BAR | *229–231 Grosvenor Road*

Popularly known as 'Daddy-O's' around the middle of the 20th century, Caulfield's Bar was situated in an area where a large number of rag dealers owned premises. Over the years it became a natural gathering spot for many of the city's rag-and-bone men and the dealers who bought from them. Since the rag-and-bone men often finished their rounds early in the day, it wasn't uncommon to find a singsong in full swing at Caulfield's in the middle of the afternoon. The bar was owned by John McKee and John Mooney before it was taken over by Thomas Caulfield in 1938. It disappeared in the early 1970s.

THE CENTRE HALF BAR | *Panton Street*

Mickey Hamill was one of the most celebrated players ever to don a jersey for Belfast Celtic, the West Belfast soccer club that enjoyed a glorious career from 1891 until 1948. His 20-year association with the club began in 1909. During that period, he also played for Manchester United (who signed him for the princely sum of £175), Glasgow Celtic, Manchester City and a club in the United States. His varied career meant that he was one of the few players to win championship medals in the English, Scottish and Irish leagues. He also captained the first Northern Ireland team to win a Home International championship in 1914.

When Hamill retired from the game, he entered the bar trade and ran the Centre Half Bar just off the Falls Road for many years. The premises had been used for the sale of drink since the 1890s, when they were owned by a spirit dealer called J. Gillen, and after the turn of the century they were run by Hugh Kane. Mickey Hamill took over the bar from Hugh Kane in 1930. The Hamill family also owned the Hamill Hotel in Great Victoria Street, which became THE BEATEN DOCKET under new ownership in 1985.

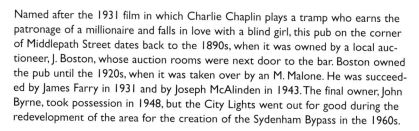

THE CITY LIGHTS | *24–26 Newtownards Road*

Named after the 1931 film in which Charlie Chaplin plays a tramp who earns the patronage of a millionaire and falls in love with a blind girl, this pub on the corner of Middlepath Street dates back to the 1890s, when it was owned by a local auctioneer, J. Boston, whose auction rooms were next door to the bar. Boston owned the pub until the 1920s, when it was taken over by an M. Malone. He was succeeded by James Farry in 1931 and by Joseph McAlinden in 1943. The final owner, John Byrne, took possession in 1948, but the City Lights went out for good during the redevelopment of the area for the creation of the Sydenham Bypass in the 1960s.

THE CLOCK BAR | *37 Donegall Road*

The Clock Bar in Sandy Row and its namesake in Connswater were both easily identified because of the distinctive wooden casks with clock faces attached, which were mounted prominently on an outside wall at each bar. Both pubs were familiar landmarks in their localities from the late 1800s.

At the turn of the century, the Sandy Row bar was owned by Moses Hunter, who was also the proprietor of several other bars in the city, including one nearby at the corner of Donegall Road and Shaftesbury Square. For a 40-year period from 1922 until the mid-1960s the Clock Bar was in the hands of W. J. Armstrong, who also owned a pub in Willow Street, off the Grosvenor Road.

The Clock Bar in Connswater was replaced in the 1960s by the New Clock Bar, owned by the Hastings family, but it has since wound down while its namesake on the Donegall Road has been transformed into the Sandy Row Rangers Supporters' Club.

THE COLLEGE ARMS | *2 Edward Street*

Situated in what was once a quiet residential area behind St Anne's Cathedral, this once-popular pub dominated the corner of Edward Street and Exchange Street West, which was described as just 'four small houses' in 1910. Formerly known as the Exchange Arms, the atmospheric little bar later changed its name to reflect its popularity with students from the nearby college in York Street. Noted for its distinctive doorway located under the overhanging corners of the building, the College Arms probably dated from around the First World War and was owned by James Joseph Heaney during the 1930s and 1940s. Joseph O'Brien ran it during the 1960s and the proprietor in the early 1970s was a J. McKenna. Today, nothing remains of the College Arms and the area is a rather sad amalgam of car parks and run-down buildings.

CRIMEA TAVERN | *207 Shankill Road*

Despite the fact that many of the allied military campaigns of the Crimean War were badly mismanaged and often resulted in pointless slaughter, they were readily commemorated in the naming of Belfast streets which were created in the years that followed the war's conclusion. On the Crumlin Road, Alma Terrace was named after the battle of the River Alma; similarly, there was an Alma Street off the Falls Road. Inkerman Terrace on the Dublin Road and Balaklava Street off the Falls Road commemorated two allied victories against the Russians in 1854 while Sevastopol Street, again off the Falls Road, was named after the lengthy and inept siege that concluded the war.

Sevastopol Street is the only one of these streets that is still in existence, but another surviving is Crimea Street, stretching from the Shankill Road to the Crumlin Road. At the corner of this street once stood the Crimea Tavern, an old Shankill bar with a long history.

The pub dates back to at least the 1860s, when it was called the Crimea Tavern and Grocery and was owned by a Mrs Elizabeth Mallon. She manned the counter until around 1880 when Susannah Mallon, presumably a daughter, took over. A long series of owners followed, including Edward Saye from the late 1890s to around 1910, John C. Moore until around 1922, Robert McGurin until 1936, and the Dobbin family – who also owned a pub at Rosemount Gardens off the Antrim Road – until 1947. At this time the tavern was purchased by the expanding Hastings group of pubs, which also included the REX BAR a few doors away and the Mountainview Tavern further up the Shankill. The Hastings ownership lasted until the mid 1960s when the bar was purchased by Samuel Crozier. After more than a century of serving up drink, however, the Crimea Tavern was consigned to the history books in 1976.

THE CROWN LIQUOR SALOON | *42 Great Victoria Street*

In a roundabout way, we probably have the Catholic Church to thank for the splendid interior of one of the finest Victorian bars in the British Isles. Up until the 1880s, the Crown was just like any other travellers' inn, unimaginatively christened the Ulster Railway Hotel and run by Felix O'Hanlon from South Armagh as a place of refreshment and accommodation for the passengers of the recently established Ulster Railway to Lisburn.

Then it was taken over by a Banbridge man, Michael Flanigan, whose son Patrick was enthusiastic about architecture and had by chance been touring Spain and Italy studying Mediterranean buildings. Patrick was inspired by what he saw and returned with great plans for his father's newly acquired bar. Soon after the purchase was made, Belfast architects E. and J. Byrne were hired to draw up the blueprints.

And this is where the Catholic Church comes in. A Catholic synod held in Co. Tipperary in 1850 had sparked a significant regeneration of the faith and churches began to spring up across the land in the ensuing years. To meet the

Elaborate Victorian stained glass doors mark the entrance to the Crown's lavatories

demand for new churches, craftsmen from all over Europe, and in particular Italy, flocked to Ireland. For the Flanigans it was too good an opportunity to miss, and several of the finest Italian craftsmen were hired to transform their grand designs into reality.

The fine exteriors of the Crown and Robinson's

The results of their labours were unveiled to Belfast's drinking public in 1885 and it seems that customers were impressed by the bar's opulent touches of stained glass and plaster mouldings; the push-button bells and mottoes like 'Love Your Country' or 'Fortune Favours the Brave' decorating the snugs. The Crown's elevated status was firmly cemented in 1946 with the release of a rather minor film called *Odd Man Out*, which starred James Mason as an IRA gunman on the run. Genuine exteriors of the bar were used in the movie, but the interior was recreated on a sound stage in Denham Studios in England. Today, most people remember the film not because of the plot or the acting, but simply because the Crown was in it.

Many famous names have stopped off at the Crown for a glass or two over the years. One of the more eloquent to visit was the Poet Laureate, Sir John Betjeman, who described the interior as 'a many-coloured cavern' and heartily approved of the snugs with doors, 'where serious drinkers can hoist their pints in contented privacy'.

The 1960s and 1970s were not kind to the Crown, however. The pub stands directly across the road from the Europa Hotel, with its unenvied distinction as the most bombed hotel in Europe, and during the worst years of the Troubles the Crown was buffeted by more than 30 blasts. By the end of the 1970s its stained

glass windows had been shattered many times, garish strip lighting had been installed and customers had all but deserted the city centre at night.

Then in 1979, the National Trust assumed ownership of the Crown – it is said that Sir John Betjeman had considerable influence in the decision – and Bass Ireland took over the management of the premises. Stills from *Odd Man Out* were used to help recreate the lost plasterwork and stained glass, gas lighting was rein-stalled and, remarkably, the moulds for the original 1885 tiles were discovered at the Ironbridge Gorge Museum in Shropshire. In 1981, almost a century after Michael Flanigan's grand liquor saloon was first unveiled, the doors of the restored Crown were thrown open once again by television newsreader Angela Rippon. And among the first to enjoy a pint at the bar was Cyril Cusack, one of the stars of *Odd Man Out*.

But the Crown's travails were far from over. Only a few years after the reopening, it was found to be riddled with dry rot and a specialist who had helped to save Brighton Pavilion from the same fate was brought over to cure the Crown's problems at a cost of around £250,000. A further £450,000 was spent in 1988 on the creation of the upstairs lounge, initially named the *Britannic* Lounge after fixtures and fittings from the *Titanic*'s sister ship – torpedoed in the Aegean in 1916 – were used in the decor. Today, the upstairs lounge has been renamed Flanigan's, in honour of the enterprising father and son whose desire to be differ-ent led to the creation of one of Belfast's most celebrated pubs.

THE CROWN TAVERN | *Crown Entry*

Few pubs in the city of Belfast can lay claim to being the birthplace of a revolution, but this long-vanished watering hole is thought to have been one of them. It is not known whether or not the founders of the Society of United Irishmen appreciated the irony of the location, but it may have been in the Crown Tavern in Crown Entry that this secret republican society was founded on 14 October 1791. Inspired by the vision of Dr William Drennan, son of the minister of Rosemary Street Presbyterian Church, a group of Belfast radicals gathered at the tavern and resolved to form an association 'to unite all Irishmen to pledge themselves to our country, and by that cordial union maintain that balance of patriotism so essential for the restoration and preservation of our liberty, and the revival of our trade'. This act in a tiny backstreet Belfast inn set in motion a chain of events that was to culminate in the ill-fated and often bloody rebellion of 1798 and which in turn led to the passing of the Act of Union that created the United Kingdom of Great Britain and Ireland in 1801.

There is, however, some dispute over the birthplace of the United Irishmen. Some say it actually took place in PEGGY BARCLAY'S TAVERN in Sugar House Entry; others say that it took place in Peggy Barclay's Tavern in Crown Entry. A third sug-gestion is that Peggy Barclay owned the Crown Tavern as well as the tavern in Sugar House Entry. Two hundred years on, it's difficult to say what the truth of it all is, but most authorities seem to agree that the United Irishmen first saw the light of day in Crown Entry and the Crown Tavern was certainly well known for its gatherings of society sympathisers around the 1798 period.

The tavern's history beyond that time is unclear, although it is known that in 1819 there were two publicans operating in Crown Entry – William Bartram at No 2 and John Stewart further along the laneway. In 1850, the only person licensed to serve drink in Crown Entry was a C. Hunter, while in 1870 Thomas Kane, who had opened the Oyster Tavern in nearby Wilson's Court some 30 years previously, was behind the counter of the Crown Shellfish Tavern. In 1880 a firm of wine and spirit merchants called the Criterion Wine Company, under the managership of J. H. Robinson, was operating from Nos 2–4, while further along the entry the Crown Dining Company operated luncheon rooms. By 1892, the only publican in Crown Entry was a Mrs Kane, who sold her pub in the early part of the 20th century to a man called O. Gallagher and he renamed it the Cave Bar.

THE CROW'S NEST | *22–26 Skipper Street*

Skipper Street, one of the oldest thoroughfares in Belfast, earned its name from the fact that masters of sailing vessels often lodged here while their ships were tied up at the quays which lined the Farset River in the middle of High Street. In 1861, the portion of Skipper Street which was later occupied by the Crow's Nest was home to two pubs. Robert Black ran a bar which stretched around the corner of Skipper Street onto High Street while next door to him was Catherine Forsyth's boarding house and spirit dealer's. Of the two, it was Black that prospered, probably because his frontage onto High Street was temptingly close to the ships' berths. He eventually took over Forsyth's pub and boarding house and by 1880 James Black, presumably Robert's son, was the landlord at 26 Skipper Street. Another member of the family, M. Black, took over before the turn of the century and he manned the counter until around 1910.

For most of the 20th century, however, the Crow's Nest was owned by the Conlan family – first by Thomas Conlan, who steered the premises through the difficult years of the First World War, and then by Mary Conlan, who remained the proprietor for 30 years before the pub's ownership was transferred to a limited company bearing the family's name. In the 1970s, P. J. Clarkin became the licensee, and then the Crow's Nest was purchased by the drinks firm Bass, which put the pub up for sale along with five other Belfast bars in 2000. After lying dormant for a while, this long-established bar has now been reopened and renamed the Custom House.

THE DEER'S HEAD | *1 Lower Garfield Street*

In 1881, the 20th President of the United States, James Abram Garfield, was assassinated and in tribute to him a street running from Smithfield to North Street was named in his honour. Four years later, at the point where Garfield Street joins North Street, John Donnelly, a wholesale and retail wine and spirit merchant, founded a new pub on this site and christened it the Deer's Head. Donnelly's bar replaced the North Star Inn, which had stood on the site some years previously, and it was just a few doors away from another old pub, the White Cross Inn, which had relocated from Castle Place. The Deer's Head has been a Croft Inns pub since the early 1970s.

DONEGALL ARMS HOTEL | Castle Place

On 16 July 1798, Henry Joy McCracken, one of the founders of the United Irishmen and a leader of the failed uprising which took place that year, spent his last night on earth in the Donegall Arms Hotel. The hotel was being used as a temporary holding place for prisoners and on the following day, Henry Joy was taken from the building, tried at the city court and executed at the gallows outside the Market House at the corner of Corn Market and High Street. "He was only a few minutes from the time he came out, till he was launched into eternity," reported the Belfast News-Letter. 'After hanging one hour, his body was given over to his friends.'

Throughout its 150-year history, the Donegall Arms was well used to playing a central role in the life of the city. In its former incarnation as the New Inn, the hotel played host to many fashionable gatherings. The Belfast Hunt met here around the time of the French Revolution and the city gentry were often to be seen wining and dining in its rooms, listening to musical recitals or lectures, or attending earnest meetings of intellectual societies. Business entrepreneurs, such as Hamilton Barr, Chimney Doctor, used the hotel facilities to advertise their services to wealthy clients: 'Hamilton Barr performs curing of smoking chimneys (no cure, no pay) upon reasonable terms, and he performs his work in the neatest manner, and doubts not that he will give satisfaction to any that employs him, as he undertakes none but them that he is sure will cure; any gentlemen that want their chimneys cured may enquire at the New Inn, Belfast, or the Sign of the Bear in Lisburn.'

The hotel was also a terminus for the Dublin coach, and often large crowds would gather outside the building whenever a coach was due so that they would be the first to hear the latest news from Dublin. Two coaches left every day at 5 am and 4 pm to make the 27-hour journey to Dublin. The Londonderry coach set off daily from the hotel at 11.30 am and arrived at its destination around 4 am the following morning.

The exact date of the foundation of the New Inn is uncertain, but it is known to have been a focal point of the city as early as 1752. The premises were rebuilt in 1786 by Thomas Sheridan and renamed the Donegall Arms. The hotel was owned by the Wilson family in the early 1800s, and in 1849 it was the scene of a banquet given by the Mayor of Belfast to mark the successful conclusion of a royal visit by Queen Victoria. The Ulster Club for leading gentlemen of the day was formed here in 1857 but moved to new premises a short distance up the street in 1862.

The Ulster Club's departure was perhaps an indicator that the Donegall Arms' heyday was past. Eight years later the hotel was absorbed by the expanding premises of John Robb and Co, who had established a drapery store a few doors further along Castle Place. By 1920 Robb's department store occupied all five

stories of Nos 1–15 Castle Place, but by 1973 it too had closed down. The buildings were severely bomb damaged during the Troubles and in 1989 Donegall
Arcade was created on the site. It's still there today and is as bustling as the
Donegall Arms ever was. However, you're unlikely to find too many chimney
doctors among its rows of shops.

DuBARRY'S | *6 Princes Street*

Few pubs in Belfast had quite the resonance of the name of DuBarry's. The dockland bar whose name was inspired by the mistress of the indolent French king,
Louis XV, was a legendary house of ill repute that survived until around 1988.
Tucked away down a narrow street leading off Queen's Square, it's said that
DuBarry's was often used as a discreet rendezvous for philandering shipowners
and their mistresses, while sailors on shore leave in search of some female company usually managed to find their way there.

Formerly the premises of J. Hampson, rope and twine manufacturer, 6 Princes
Street was taken over by a spirit dealer named William Gardiner sometime before
1870. In the 1890s, the licence was assumed by J. Tiernan, who was succeeded by a
Mrs E. Tiernan in the 1920s. During the Second World War the owner was a P.
Daly, while just around the corner was Hendron's Bar, where a young and innocent
Joe Hendron – later to serve as West Belfast MP – found himself having to give
directions to DuBarry's on many occasions.

'I remember there were always young ladies hanging out in DuBarry's next
door,' he recalled. 'Some American soldiers once asked me were there any women.
Not realising what he meant, I pointed him in the direction of DuBarry's and he
gave me chewing gum.'

It's also recorded that in the 1940s, the brother of celebrated artist Stanley
Spencer played honky-tonk piano in DuBarry's. It may have been around this time
that the inspired choice of name was first applied to the premises, although it
doesn't appear in the *Belfast Street Directory* until 1953, when the bar was owned
by a P. O'Hara. No 4 Princes Street, also owned by Mr O'Hara, was the exotically
titled Rue Plumet cocktail lounge from the early 1950s until the late 1970s, when
it became, rather more prosaically, the rear of a Chinese takeaway.

THE DUKE INN | *156 Old Lodge Road*

A pub with no known connections to nobility, but rather named after the owner's
hope that customers would 'juke in' for a drink. The Old Lodge Road, now obliterated from the map of Belfast by redevelopment, was renowned for its abundance
of small family-run bars and for many years the Duke Inn was one of them. Over
the years, however, it gained something of a reputation as a bar frequented by
local prostitutes.

There had been premises serving drink at the corner of Foreman Street since
at least 1860, when Edward Donnelly was the licensee. Ten years later, No 156 and
next door were run by McKeown and Crawford, grocers and spirit dealers, and in

the 1890s the business was run by a Mr T. Girvan. There was a succession of owners in the early 20th century and in the period from 1943–45 it was sold three times, ending up in the hands of Edward Farwell in 1945.

In 1958, James and Mary Diver took out a lease on the premises for the sum of £8 per week, continuing a family tradition which began in the 1920s with a spirit grocery business. They ran the bar until 1977, and in 1978 the family bought ROBINSON'S BAR from Barney O'Neill, currently the owner of the Garrick. The Diver family now owns WHITE'S TAVERN, the MONICO BAR and THE BEATEN DOCKET.

THE DUKE OF YORK | *7–11 Commercial Court*

Tucked away down a narrow entry off Donegall Street – Belfast's equivalent of Fleet Street – the Duke of York's proximity to so many of the city's newspaper offices has made it a natural haunt for journalists throughout its long history. Indeed, the pub has outlived many of the publications that once employed its most devoted customers. Remember the *Ulster Echo*, anyone? Or the *Morning News*? These were just two newspapers that were once published from offices conveniently located just a few doors away. Another was the *Ulster Examiner*, later to become the *Irish Weekly*, which was founded by Dr Dorrian, the Bishop of Down and Connor, in this busy cobbled entry in 1868. Just around the corner on Donegall Street were the offices of the *News Letter*, a hundred yards in the other direction was the *Northern Whig*. All of them are gone. The *News Letter* is the only one of these papers still being published, but no longer in Donegall Street.

Jostling with the journos for space at the bar over the years have been poets and politicians, judges and trades unionists, writers and raconteurs. Gerry Fitt and Paddy Devlin supped alongside celebrated *News Letter* columnist Ralph 'Bud' Bossence and novelist Sam Hanna Bell. Others recall senior Stormont civil servants and leading republicans mingling among the regulars.

The pub has a unique claim to be the home of Belfast's first boxing club. Tom Boyce's Boxing Saloon was said to have been formed upstairs at The Duke of York sometime during the first half of the 19th century. Many years later, sparring of a more verbal kind was the order of the day when the Belfast branch of the National Union of Journalists was formed in those same upstairs rooms.

There has been a pub on this site since about 1810, and in common with most other pubs in the city, it has undergone many changes of name and owner since that time. At one point it was known as the Widow's; at another time it was called the Gluepot, apparently because customers believed it was so difficult to extract themselves from it. It wasn't until 1917, however, that the name of the Duke of York appeared for the first time in the *Belfast Street Directory*. For a while, the bar was owned by a former submarine commander, who salvaged two portholes from a ship which caught fire in Belfast Lough and installed them in the wall separating the public bar from the lounge. Apparently, the eccentric ex-mariner also used to serve drinks wearing a gas mask on occasions.

One of the longest spells of ownership was that of the Keaveney family, who took over The Duke of York in 1938 and ran it for 35 years. Publican Jimmy

The façade of The Duke of York, in cobbled Commercial Court

Keaveney recalls that one of his first customers, an elderly lady called Maggie Magennis, was the last person to pay him for a drink with gold. She presented a half-sovereign as payment for the drink and when Jimmy pointed out that the coin

was worth more than its face value, she told him to take the price of the drink out of whatever the coin was worth.

Gerry Adams, President of Sinn Féin, worked as a barman in The Duke of York in the mid-1960s and in his autobiography he recalls it as 'a small, picturesque, low-ceilinged pub with no ventilation; it had a long bar, brass rails, swing doors, fine oak and good cartoons on the walls'.

Writer Sam McAughtry maintained that there were three classes of customer in the Duke of York in the 1960s, and each had their own bar. The smallest bar was populated by shipyard workers who sang their own versions of popular songs of the day, peppering them with the names of well-known shipyard characters; the public bar resounded to barbers' shop-style music, with a prominent local trades unionist leading the chorus; while in the lounge, where the political activists gathered, 'they were inclined to go in for the Percy French stuff'.

Some modernisation was carried out to the Duke of York in the mid-1960s, but on the night of 14 June 1973, the building took the full force of a massive bomb explosion and had to be completely demolished. Three years later, however, the bar was revived by Croft Inns Ltd – the owner of a number of pubs through-out the city – and in a fitting nod to its journalistic associations, a number of photographs taken by freelance press photographer Eddie Dineen were used to help recreate the interior of the bar.

EGLANTINE INN | *32 Malone Road*

Affectionately known as 'The Egg' by generations of students from nearby Queen's University – who no doubt would agree with the author of a Belfast pub guide in the 1960s when he said 'the atmosphere is conducive to enjoyable drinking' – the Eglantine Inn has gone through many changes in appearance over the last century.

The inn was originally designed in 1898 by E. and J. Byrne, who had been the architects for the revamped CROWN LIQUOR SALOON in Great Victoria Street some 13 years previously. It's said that the premises were an old posting inn where patrons were able to hire all sorts of horse-drawn carriages to take them on pleasure trips through the open countryside nearby.

The Eglantine Inn once changed hands for the princely sum of £18,500. This was just after the Second World War, when Miss Una Burns paid the cash to wine and spirit merchant Edward J. McLean, who had owned the place since the 1930s.

THE ELBOW ROOM | *3–5 Dublin Road*

Bought by the Lavery family from Isaac Clark in 1919, this well-known bar was to become the scene of one of the most significant literary encounters in post-war Northern Ireland. It was 1958, and by that time the Elbow had already acquired a reputation as a place where theatre folk, writers and actors met, since the BBC was just across the road and the Group Theatre was only a few hundred yards away. Mingling with the crowd on this particular night was the actor/director James Ellis, who at that time was a leading light in the Group company, and a forceful young playwright named Sam Thompson. The writer accosted Ellis and accused the Group of refusing to touch his new play, *Over the Bridge*. The drama was a stark tale of sectarianism in the Belfast shipyards, which the Board of the Group Theatre had deemed too hot to handle. But Ellis read it and liked it. He and others pressed the Board to stage the play, but they refused to budge.

Over the Bridge became a literary *cause célèbre*; its supporters resigned from the Group, formed their own company and mounted a production at the Empire Theatre. The play ran for six weeks to packed houses and the cast included both Ellis and Thompson, as well as J. G. Devlin, Joseph Tomelty, Harry Towb and James Boyce.

No doubt the encounter between James Ellis and Sam Thompson was one of many fruitful meetings which took place at the Elbow Room in the 1950s and 1960s. Among many other well-known figures from the literary scene of that era who frequented the Elbow were the celebrated actor, director and impresario Tyrone Guthrie, and Sam Hanna Bell, author of *December Bride*, *A Man Flourishing* and *The Hollow Ball*.

The first pub on the site of the Elbow Room was built in 1864, and the premises were previously known as the Windsor Castle and the Dublin Bridge Hotel. The Elbow Room was elbowed out in 1985 by a road-widening scheme and in the 1990s the name was adopted by a complex of bars further up the Dublin Road.

THE ELECTRIC BAR | *66 Bridge End*

It is said that this long-standing east Belfast pub was given its name in honour of the electrification of the Belfast tram system – a long overdue civic project which eventually got underway in 1905. However, it's possible that the real reason for the name may be a little more mundane, since not far from Bridge End an Electric Street once ran from Clifford Street to Magnetic Street. However, it was the bar's final name – the Talk of the Town – that will probably be the most familiar today.

The Electric Bar was serving drink in Bridge End well before the end of the 19th century, when a William McConvey was the owner. He was succeeded in 1915 by John Henry Branagh, who ran the place for nearly 30 years. Then John Rogan took over in 1942 and he was still behind the counter in the late 1960s. For a brief year the pub became known as the Jack McNorrie Cabaret before being rechristened the Talk of the Town in 1969. Proclaiming itself as 'Belfast's leading nightspot', the bar certainly lived up to its name. Major English and European acts were attracted to the venue and Roy Walker – later a TV star in his own right – was the resident compere. Another local comedian to regularly grace the Talk of the Town stage was Frank Carson.

A guide to Belfast pubs in the early 1970s declared: 'The Talk of the Town is one of the largest cabaret clubs in Northern Ireland and is the haunt of many a Belfast man wishing to enjoy a good night's entertainment. The wood panelling of both wall and ceiling, and unusual ultraviolet lighting all combine to give a very genial atmosphere.'

The Talk of the Town's reign as a cabaret hotspot was glorious but brief. By 1973, the Electric Bar had lost its spark and all that remained of the city's leading nightclub was a bare patch of vacant ground.

ELEPHANT BAR | *140 North Street*

Though this bar disappeared in the 1980s, its most distinctive feature, a five feet-high grey wooden elephant, is still visible in North Street today. The Elephant Buildings on the corner of Winetavern Street were believed to have been built just before the end of the 19th century, although it is said that the elephant itself is older still. The reason for the elephant is unclear – some sources say that a similar animal stands guard over a pub doorway in Dublin – although the most likely explanation is that it was a gimmick to make this bar stand out from its competi-

The south side of Upper North Street during street widening in 1894, looking west and showing the Elephant Bar (Welch Collection, Ulster Museum)

tors in North Street. And there were certainly many of those. In 1819, for example, in addition to the four spirit dealers that operated in North Street, there was the King's Arms at No 45, Martin's Tavern at No 47, the Wheatsheaf at No 76, the Buck at No 93, the Hare and Hounds at No 99, William Vint's at No 104, the Red Cow at No 126, the Horse Inn at No 132, William Hunter, publican and dealer in hides, at No 154, the Eagle at No 160, Samuel Duffield's at No 164 and James Sheals' at No 177.

In the 1960s and 1970s the Elephant Bar was run by Charles Farrell, whose family had owned the premises since the mid-1930s. A plaque bearing his name was inserted beneath the elephant sculpture and remained there for many years. The survivor of many nearby bomb blasts during the Troubles, the elephant now stands guard at the entrance to an off-licence.

THE EMPIRE MUSIC HALL | 40–42 Botanic Avenue

With its origins in the late 1980s, the Empire isn't a very old bar, but it does have the distinction of being Belfast's only pub to be housed in a former church – and it also has a resident ghost.

Looking down on the main bar area of the Empire

Named after the city's most famous music hall – the Empire Theatre of Varieties opened in Victoria Square in 1891 and packed in the crowds for 70 years – the Botanic Avenue bar was established in a derelict Reformed Presbyterian Church built around the 1870s. Following in the footsteps of its namesake, the Empire has become a popular entertainment venue, and the comedy club established here has provided a launching pad for the careers of Patrick Kielty and a number of other popular comics.

It has been claimed that since the old church did not have an adjoining cemetery, some people were buried in a crypt under the building, and the stern Victorian ghosts, it seems, do not approve of drink being served on the floors above. Staff at the Empire have reported rows of glasses smashing onto the floor for no reason, the sound of footsteps on an empty dance floor, internal phones that can't take incoming calls suddenly ringing late at night, and hand-driers starting up by themselves in empty toilets. The Empire's manager told an interviewer in 1997: 'Some staff just couldn't take it any more and left us; others refuse to come up here to the music hall after closing time'. The Empire's eerie goings-on may have given staff the jitters, but there's no sign of the pub refusing to serve spirits.

THE ERRIGLE INN | *320 Ormeau Road*

Now famous throughout the city for the quality of its musical acts – Van Morrison and Georgie Fame are just some of the many performers who have played there – the Errigle Inn was the first public house in Belfast to be granted an entertainments licence. The licence was awarded in 1967 after a turbulent application process which saw opposition put forward by such odd allies as the Northern Ireland Ballrooms' Association and the Ulster Christian Council for Temperance and Social Welfare.

In a hearing before Belfast Corporation's Police Committee, the Ballrooms' Association representative claimed that pubs with entertainment would be unfair competition for the dance halls, but he was assured by the city fathers that "no dancing would be allowed in the public houses granted a licence". After much deliberation, the licence was approved by the slim margin of five votes to two, paving the way for a flood of similar applications. Within a fortnight of the Errigle's success, a dozen other bars around the city had applied for their own entertainment licences.

The campaign to obtain the city's first ever entertainment licence for the Errigle Inn was waged by its owner, Thomas McGurran, who had purchased the premises for £12,000 from his employer, Charles McQuade, in 1944. McQuade had bought the bar for £2,400 some years beforehand from the previous owner, a Miss Black, who was the proprietor at least until 1922. In earlier times, the Errigle was known as the Old Ballynafeigh Inn, and a painting of the bar in its former days, by the celebrated Ulster artist Frank McKelvey, is in the Ulster Museum's collection.

Back in the 1930s, the Errigle had its own garden with apple and plum trees, but in the 1950s and 1960s trees of a very different kind were incorporated into the bar. Situated upstairs were the Marble Cedar Lounge – named after the special wood imported from America for wall panelling – and the Arbele Lounge, featuring arbele wood imported from South Africa, which previously had never been seen anywhere in Ireland.

The Errigle Inn has continued to evolve over the years. In anticipation of the granting of its entertainment licence in 1967, a new upstairs lounge, the 19th Hole, was created, while in 1985 the bar's roof garden was a novelty attraction. Then in 1998 an extensive facelift was carried out and the downstairs bar was renamed Tom McGurran's Bar – in honour of the man who blazed the trail for pub entertainment in Belfast.

THE FARMERS' REST | *93–95 Castlereagh Street*

Dominating the junction of Castlereagh Street and Templemore Avenue with its huge illuminated sign advertising White Horse Whisky, the Farmers' Rest was so called because of its popularity with farmers returning home to the Castlereagh Hills after a day at the Belfast markets. The bar was given its name by an owner called H. Rooney, who ran the place in the 1890s, although it had been a popular watering hole for at least 20 years before that. The McMahon family were proprietors for a 50-year period stretching from 1911 and in the 1970s it was bought by the former footballer Warren Feeney. A guidebook called *Wine and Dine in Northern Ireland*, published in 1970, declared simply: 'It is a landmark in the district and probably also the best bar'.

JOHN FETHERSTON'S | *49 Ann Street*

The much-frequented tavern of John Fetherston's was situated at the corner of Ann Street and Upper Church Lane and for a time it was one of the many premises in Ann Street which offered booking facilities for passenger coaches to North Down and the Ards Peninsula. Fetherston's was established in the 1840s as a wine and spirit dealer and acted as the main Belfast agent for the Cairnes and Son brewery of Drogheda. The building later became known for a more sedate form of liquid refreshment when it was occupied in the 1890s by the tea-importing business of S. D. Bell.

THE FORT BAR | *25 Springfield Road*

Dating back to around 1885, the Fort was owned in its early days by O. Crilly, publican and grocer. It was later run by the McGuigan family for a period of 77 years, after which the Maguire family took over and now it is known as Gilmartin's. A beautifully ornate bar with snugs, it remains a popular local rendezvous. There is a story that a fine old mahogany cabinet behind the bar once caught the eye of a wealthy American who offered to hand over £10,000 on the spot for it. The offer, apparently, was refused.

THE FOUNTAIN TAVERN | *16–20 Fountain Street*

Formerly the location of Fountain Street National School, the first tavern at this site was the Fountain Bar, which was established at the tail end of the 19th century and run by Sarah Little. The bar survived until the Second World War, when it was severely damaged during the Blitz of 1941 and had to be demolished. The Convery family, who had owned the bar before the war, rebuilt the premises

The Fountain Tavern with two old water pumps marking the front entrance

in 1955. In 1972, they were purchased along with KELLY'S CELLARS from B. O'Kane and Company by the current owners, Croft Inns.

THE FOUR IN HAND | *116–118 Lisburn Road*

The origins of the Four in Hand date back to a time when it stood in open countryside and provided a convenient refreshment stop for travellers journeying between Belfast and Lisburn. The bar's name is a tribute to its long-gone days as a coaching inn – a 'four in hand' was a coach pulled by four horses – and depictions of various types of horse-drawn transport have been a prominent feature of the bar's decor for many years. The longest-serving owners of the premises were J. and J. Hunter, who purchased the pub around 1922 from the previous owner, John McAlister, and remained the proprietors for the next half century. The drinks giant Bass later purchased the bar but sold it again in 2000, along with five other Belfast pubs – the Glenowen Inn, the CROW'S NEST, the Elms, the Ben Madigan and the Belmont. For many years, one of the most notable attractions on display inside the pub was a forged 30-shilling note made payable by the Belfast Bank and dated

1818. Sometime during the 1970s or 1980s the banknote vanished, though it seems unlikely that anyone tried to cash it. The pub is now called Ryan's Bar & Grill.

THE FRONT PAGE | *106–108 Donegall Street*

No prizes for guessing how this bar got its name. Located on the corner of Union Street, just across the road from the offices of the *Irish News* and a short distance from the *Belfast Telegraph*, it has been a popular refreshment stop with journalists and newspaper workers for many years. Established in the latter half of the 19th century on the site of what was previously Miss Alderdice's milliner's shop and before that James King's Horse Bazaar and Veterinary Establishment, the bar was owned by the Rogers family for a period of around 70 years.

It was bought by Michael Rogers sometime before 1910 and he continued to run the premises until the late 1950s when the reins were passed on to Miss Mary Rogers. Ten years later, she added a lounge to the premises, but not without long deliberation beforehand. A guide to Belfast hostelries published in 1967 noted: 'Miss Rogers and her manager, Mr Kilfeather, were reluctant to make any alterations which would have spoiled the character of the bar, but, to cater for the wishes of those who prefer a smaller, more intimate place to drink, they have recently added a very pleasing lounge'. In the middle of the 19th century, Dr Barter's Turkish Baths were established next door to the bar and continued to operate until the 1930s.

THE GARRICK | *29 Chichester Street*

It has been said that the famous 18th-century Shakespearean actor David Garrick – who coincidentally was involved in the wine trade before he succumbed to the lure of the stage – once visited this bar for a drink, but that seems a highly unlikely notion. Garrick did visit Ireland on a few occasions, mostly performing in Dublin, but he died in 1779, around a century before the Garrick bar was founded. It's possible, however, that the name could have been inspired by the Garrick Club, a fashionable London rendezvous which was founded in 1831 as a place where 'actors and men of education and refinement might meet on equal terms'. The Garrick Club was a favourite watering hole of the author William Thackeray, who visited Belfast in 1842 and for all we know may have planted the suggestion in someone's head at that time.

Around the time of Thackeray's visit, the site of the Garrick was occupied by the marble and stone yard of William Low, who later ran a unique combined enterprise of spirit dealer and cement merchant in Victoria Square on the site of what is now THE KITCHEN BAR. At some point during the 30 years that followed, a tavern was established at the corner of Chichester Street and Montgomery Street, and in 1870 McCauley, McCashin and Co, who described themselves as rectifying distillers and wine and spirit merchants, were dispensing drink at this location.

The Garrick name was in use by 1892 at the latest, when W. J. McCoy ran the Garrick Bar and Billiard Room. Before the turn of the century, the bar became the

The Garrick, as it appeared in the 1930s (from the Hogg Collection, Ulster Museum)

second licensed premises to be acquired by the burgeoning partnership of Braithwaite and McCann and for many years served as the firm's head office in the city.

Currently owned by the O'Neill family, who were proprietors of ROBINSON'S in Great Victoria Street for some years, the bar's renovated interior is a smart combination of tiling and woodwork, which has earned the owners the accolade of Belfast's Best Kept Small Building on a number of occasions.

THE GIN PALACE | *92 Royal Avenue*

Although this pub had a short life of not much more than 25 years, it became one of Belfast's best-known bars in the early part of the 20th century, chiefly because of its dominant position on the corner of Royal Avenue and North Street. It's said that there was a bar on this site as early as 1870, but it was in 1899 that Palace Chambers – the three-storey building which curved around this corner – was home to the Gin Palace owned by publican John J. Connolly.

By 1907, however, the premises were in the hands of Hugh Donaghy, wine and spirit dealer, and the following year he sold them to James Armstrong, a publican who also owned bars in Ann Street and North Street. Armstrong, whose name was emblazoned in eight-feet high letters perched on the top of the building, managed the premises throughout the dry years of the First World War but by 1921 he too had sold up. An entry in the 1922 *Belfast Street Directory* declared that the site was to be 'new premises for the Bank of Ireland' and the art deco building that was erected there over the next few years still dominates this landmark corner today.

THE GLOBE TAVERN | *4 Joy's Entry*

Joy's Entry, a narrow lane running from Ann Street to High Street, was named after Henry Joy, a grandson of the founder of the *Belfast News Letter*, Francis Joy, who became editor of the paper in 1789 and printed it in premises in this laneway during the early 1800s. Tradition has it that the Globe Tavern was at one time owned by an Admiral and was a favourite haunt of sailors whose ships were tied up at the quays along High Street. Records show that a publican named John Byrne was serving drink from 4 Joy's Entry in 1892, and before the end of the century the bar had adopted the name of the Globe. Around 1910 the premises also included the Globe Billiard Rooms and from the 1920s onwards, the restaurant facilities were expanded and the pub became known as the Globe Luncheon Bar. It is now called O'Neill's Café Bar

GOLDEN GATE BAR | *87 Peter's Hill*

This long-disappeared bar on the corner of Townsend Street probably earned its exotic San Franciscan name to the fact that it was close to Lower California Street, which ran from Peter's Hill to the Old Lodge Road. There was also a California Street, which connected the Old Lodge Road with Wall Street. Like the Golden Gate Bar, both these streets have been swallowed up by redevelopment, but there is a still a California Close in the area today.

THE GREAT EASTERN | *273 Newtownards Road*

Since many bars on the Newtownards Road were located just the toss of a rivet from the heart of Belfast's shipbuilding industry, it was not unnatural for landlords to choose the name of a ship for their premises. So when a pub opened its doors at 273 Newtownards Road in the 1880s, the owner decided to honour Isambard Kingdom Brunel's mighty iron steamship, the *Great Eastern*, which was built in London in 1858. The Belfast bar was one of a number throughout the British Isles given that name, which although popular, was an odd choice, since the *Great Eastern* was widely regarded as a jinxed vessel that seemed to attract misfortune wherever it went.

No such misfortune attached itself to the Great Eastern on the Newtownards Road, however. Owned by an M. Pritchard at the turn of the century, the bar was taken over in 1910 by B. McMahon. By 1922 the bar was in the hands of James Harrison, who sold it to Bernard Hillen in the early 1930s. At the end of the Second World War, Hillen accepted an offer of £13,000 for the bar from Jessie C. Hastings, and her acquisition of the bar meant that the Hastings family owned a total of five pubs on the Newtownards Road at that time. Later owners of the Great Eastern included W. T. Amery in the 1950s and Patrick Brennan, who was also the proprietor of PAT'S BAR across the Lagan in Princes Dock Street, in the 1960s.

Over the years the pub has changed its name a couple of times, being variously known as the Red Hand Bar and the Ulster Arms. After a grant-aided renovation programme, however, the name was changed back to the original Great Eastern in the 1970s by the then owners, the Allen Brothers. The present proprietors, Alan Irvine and Robert Townsley, have refurbished the bar twice since then.

HATFIELD HOUSE | *130 Ormeau Road*

Recently restored to its former glory, the splendidly ornate façade of this notable South Belfast bar is topped by a curving metalwork sign bearing the names of Braithwaite and McCann, spirit merchants. It is one of the few visible reminders of a pub chain that was once a major player in the city's licensed trade and it is fitting that the sign is attached to this pub, since the Hatfield was the partnership's very first premises.

The first bar on this site is supposed to date back to at least 1873, although it appears that Braithwaite and McCann's ownership did not begin until the late 1880s or early 1890s, when it was a spirit grocers situated at 3 Hatfield Terrace. The business obviously thrived, for by 1899 the pair had enough capital to purchase the Red Lion further up the Ormeau Road and THE GARRICK in Chichester Street. By 1910 Braithwaite and McCann had added THE STORE BAR at 21 Church Lane and a spirit grocers at the corner of India Street and Botanic Avenue to their expanding empire. Later THE ULSTER TAVERN in Chichester Street was also bought up, and at its height the partnership owned 15 bars around the city.

Hatfield House boasts an ornate late Victorian façade

During the 1960s, the firm dropped the name of Braithwaite and became known simply as McCann Ltd. It linked up with the Belfast bottling firm of Morton and Co, which had merged with the English brewery, Thwaites of Blackburn, to introduce the Lancashire firm's Star Keg beer into Northern Ireland. In the early 1970s, Mortons began buying up Belfast pubs on Thwaites' behalf and by 1974 they had spent over £5 million building up a network of 27 pubs that included the McCann premises. Today, all the surviving Braithwaite and McCann premises are independently owned.

The Hatfield's lavish craftsmanship inside and out bears testament to the considerable care which Braithwaite and McCann took over the look of their premises. One unusual feature of the premises was a door which at one time connected the bar with a house situated between it and the North of Ireland Cricket Club's ground. This was the dental and medical practice of brothers Robert and Harold Martin and it's said that patients would often be seen using this quick escape route from the surgery to obtain a painkiller or two in the Hatfield.

THE HERCULES BAR | *61–63 Castle Street*

At first glance it might seem that the publican who named this bar was inspired by heroic deeds from Greek mythology, but the real inspiration was in fact a lot closer to home. Royal Avenue, just around the corner from Castle Street, was formerly known as Hercules Street – an area that was virtually wall-to-wall butchers' shops at one time, and was also considered to be one of the scruffiest and most violent parts of the city. This can't have pleased the man after whom the street was named, Sir Hercules Langford, a leading Belfast citizen whose family also gave their name to Langford Lodge on the shores of Lough Neagh.

The bar was founded in 1875 on the site of two commercial premises, William McCormick, house and land agent, and S. Maguire and Co., jewellery importers, by Patrick McGlade, who with his brother Francis went on to establish MCGLADE'S BAR in Donegall Street and later owned many other premises in the city. The Hercules name dates back to at least the beginning of the 20th century, when the premises were known as the Hercules Wine and Spirit Stores. For a short time in the 1970s, the bar was given the rather dowdy name of the Brown Cow.

THE HOLE IN THE WALL | *1-3 Baltic Avenue*

It is difficult to imagine today, but when the first inn at this busy Antrim Road location opened its doors, there was little but open country all around. It is not clear exactly when the inn was founded, but it was at a time when Belfast was still relatively small and today's built-up streets in the north of the city could scarcely be imagined. The inn was for a number of years a popular stopping-off point for travellers, although it also acquired a reputation as a spot frequented by highwaymen. It is said that customers were often relieved of their valuables as they left the tavern to head for the city.

In the 19th century, the city gradually spread out to meet the inn, which by 1892 was known as The Shaftesbury Arms and owned by Patrick Leonard. In 1899 the bar was taken over by Rooney Bros, a family firm that retained ownership of the bar for 80 years. The pub's change of name to The Hole in the Wall first appeared in the *Belfast Street Directory* in 1967.

THE INTERNATIONAL HOTEL | *6–7 Donegall Square South*

In the mid-1960s increasing calls for changes to the electoral system and an end to discrimination against Catholics in the allocation of council houses and employment led to the formation of the Northern Ireland Civil Rights Association. Its inaugural meeting was held in the International Hotel on 29 January 1967, and was attended by over 100 delegates from a broad spectrum of pressure groups and representatives of all Northern Ireland's political parties. Most of the aims of the civil rights movement were achieved – universal suffrage was introduced in 1969, the Housing Executive was established in 1971 and the Fair Employment Agency was created in 1976 – but a series of marches and counter-marches in the years

'The International', just after it closed its doors in 1975

following the Association's formation descended into violent confrontation and provided a curtain-raiser for the Troubles of 1969 onwards.

And it was the Troubles that put an end to the International Hotel. Formerly called the Union Hotel, it had been built around the turn of the century and was renamed the International in 1960. Like so many city centre premises, it bore the brunt of several bomb attacks in the early 1970s, and when the almost nightly violence drove people away from the heart of Belfast during the hours of darkness, the hotel could no longer stay in business.

The International closed its doors for the last time on 18 May 1975, and although the 30 staff were paid off, the management said the hotel bar would remain open. This arrangement did not last long, however, and in November of that year, Belfast City Council took a controversial decision to buy the property for £220,000 and convert it into offices and a canteen. After owning the building for a number of years, the council sold the site to a developer.

Belfast writer Glenn Patterson's 1999 novel, *The International*, focuses on the eccentric – and fictional – customers of the hotel's Blue Bar in 1967.

JUBILEE BAR | *56 Cromac Street*

Also known as the Golden Jubilee Bar, this colourful watering hole was established on the site of premises owned by Frank McGlade, who later opened McGLADE's BAR in Donegall Street with his brother Patrick. In 1870 Frank ran a wholesale grocery business, a wine and spirit merchants, and a bottling establishment at 56 Cromac Street. A century later, the Jubilee Bar on that same site was firmly established as one of the entertainment hotspots of the city. Run by Des Gillespie, it hosted folk bands on Mondays and Wednesdays, jazz on Tuesdays and Fridays (the Belfast Jazz Society was formed here in 1966) and a Singalong with Sammy at the end of the week. And if that wasn't enough, the bar also had its own honky-tonk piano to entertain customers. Pub historian J. J. Tohill recalls that a highlight of the Jubilee was the lavishly decorated Omar Khayyam room, featuring a gold colour scheme and illustrated passages from the Persian poet's often-quoted *Rubaiyat* on the walls, while a 1970s guide to the city's pubs noted that an important feature of the bar was that you could buy 'one of the best baps in Belfast' there.

THE JUNCTION ARMS | *124 Mountpottinger Road*

The sign above the door may have said 'The Junction Arms', but to everyone who knew of this east Belfast pub it was Holy Joe's. The pub earned its nickname from the fact that the owner was one of the few pub landlords who would insist that shipyard workers fresh from their shift went home and gave their wages to their wives before he would serve them a drink.

Holy Joe was probably Joseph P. O'Connor, who owned The Junction Arms from 1936 until at least the mid 1960s. Some of those who frequented the long-disappeared bar maintain that the reason Holy Joe was so conscientious about his customers' welfare was that he had originally trained for the priesthood!

The Junction Arms earned its name from the fact that it was located at the junction of Mountpottinger Road and Albertbridge Road, though some customers also referred to the bar as Murray's. This was because it was owned for over 25 years by Charles Murray, who was the proprietor of a number of pubs in that area during the early years of the 20th century.

KELLY'S CELLARS | *30 Bank Street*

There may be some dispute over its age – it is claimed that this bar was founded in 1720, although many experts reckon that it didn't open its doors until 1780 – but there is little argument over the assertion that Kelly's Cellars is the oldest surviving continually run pub in Belfast. Formerly a spirit merchants called Kelly's Stores, the bar may have changed in many ways from its original appearance, but its vaulted interior still retains more than a whiff of its long and colourful past.

Kelly's used to supply refreshment to members of the Society of United Irishmen when they held secret meetings on the premises to plot the rebellion of 1798, and it's said that Henry Joy McCracken, one of the Society's founders, once

The clock in Kelly's Cellars claims an early 18th-century foundation

hid under the counter to evade pursuing redcoats. The old low counter that concealed McCracken was apparently still there in 1961, although it has since been replaced at least twice.

In the early part of this century, the well-known Nationalist politician Joe Devlin – 'Wee Joe' as he became known – was the bar manager at Kelly's. Devlin was a remarkable figure; he became an MP in 1902 and held the West Belfast seat from 1906 until his death in 1934. During that time, he was instrumental in reviving the Ancient Order of Hibernians in 1905, defeated Eamon de Valera in the election of 1918 and was Belfast's only nationalist representative at Stormont in 1921. Such was his broad appeal to the city's working classes that when Wee Joe died, a thousand delegates at the AGM of the Ulster Unionist Labour Association stood in silent tribute to him.

In his Belfast memoir, *As I Roved Out*, writer Cathal O'Byrne recalled the loft of Kelly's Cellars being used as a store for the equipment of medical practitioner and amateur showman Dr Thomas Corry of Chichester Street. In the latter half of the 19th century, Dr Corry was celebrated for his dioramas – the precursor of motion pictures – which consisted of giant moving rolls of canvas on which were painted depictions of Irish life and local scenery from Killarney to the Giant's Causeway.

The most detailed recollections of Kelly's come from historian J. J. Tohill, whose father, James Tohill, head of the wine firm Tohill Vino, purchased the premises in 1942 – just a year after the bar was damaged in the Blitz. J. J. Tohill believed that for many years Kelly's was 'the only daytime men-only bar in Ireland', although there was a large snug specially set aside for women. 'I could never understand why,' said Tohill, 'but ladies never had equal status in Kelly's, even when the two lounges were opened upstairs, father not only had a commissionaire on the door, but a notice stating quite clearly that ladies would be refused admittance unless accompanied by a gentleman'.

The first upstairs 'cocktail lounge' was opened in 1948 and its chief attraction was a ceiling mural commissioned at a cost of £600 and painted by the celebrated artist Sydney Smith, who was acclaimed for his paintings of Belfast during the Second World War. Sadly Smith's mural, a homage to Bacchus, the Greek god of wine, was painted over some years later. In 1954, a second lounge, called the Tudor Lounge, was created and the opening ceremony was carried out by the international goalkeeper Frank Swift, who died four years later in the Munich air disaster.

In 1961, Kelly's Cellars was sold for what was then a record price of £43,000 to B. O'Kane and Company. The O'Kanes were the owners of the Glenshesk Inn on the corner of King Street and Castle Street, which had been modernised by Bernard O'Kane in 1929 and subsequently managed by his son, Kevin O'Kane. After owning Kelly's Cellars for 11 years, the O'Kane family sold the premises to Croft Inns, which purchased the FOUNTAIN TAVERN at the same time.

Throughout the bar's long history, many famous people have downed a glass or two in Kelly's Cellars. A visitor's book was created in the early 1950s and among the signatures in its pages are those of Stanley Matthews, Peter Doherty, Nat Lofthouse, Jock Stein, Bill Shankly and Matt Busby from the world of soccer, boxers Sonny Liston, Floyd Patterson and Rinty Monaghan, movie actor Stephen Boyd, poet Louis MacNeice, artist William Conor, and local theatre actors Joseph Tomelty, Harold Goldblatt and J. G. Devlin. Few other bars in Belfast could ever boast such a distinguished line-up of customers.

THE KITCHEN BAR | *16 Victoria Square*

Victoria Square was buzzing with excitement on the night of Monday 16 November 1896. Dan Lowrey, the celebrated impresario, had booked a very special act to appear at his Empire Theatre of Varieties, next door to The Kitchen Bar. Direct from France came the Lumière brothers, who less than 12 months earlier had astounded Paris with their exhibition of moving pictures. Their show in the Empire lasted only 15 minutes or so, consisting of a series of one-minute films showing quite mundane things like a baby being fed and young swimmers diving into the sea, but Belfast had never seen anything quite like it. Afterwards, no doubt, many of the patrons of the Empire – and maybe even the Lumière brothers them-selves – adjourned to the Kitchen to discuss the birth of the movies in Belfast.

Situated at the corner of Telfair's Entry, between the music hall and the head-quarters of the distilling firm, Holywood and Donnelly (famous at the time for their Banquet Whiskey), The Kitchen Bar was run in 1896 by Thomas Conlan, who was also the proprietor of licensed premises at 49–51 Victoria Square. Another bar, run by N. Macarthur, was located at Nos 39–41. Nearby was the head office

The Kitchen Bar has been on the corner of Telfair's Entry and Victoria Square for almost a century and a half

of Cantrell and Cochrane, aerated water manufacturers, and the Irish Distillery grain store. In an apparent attempt to counteract the attraction of so many pubs and drinks firms gathered in one place, the Irish Temperance League maintained a coffee stand in the square for many years.

It is claimed that The Kitchen Bar was founded in 1859, although the 1861 *Belfast Street Directory* shows no listing for a pub anywhere in the square. By 1870, however, the corner of Telfair's Entry and Victoria Square was occupied by William Low, whose unusual combination of trades included spirit merchant and dealer in cement and alabaster. The name of the Kitchen Bar appears in the street directory for the first time in 1880, when it was owned by a spirit dealer named Rose Connor. At that time, the bar was not exactly on the corner of Telfair's Entry, however – that site was occupied by the bonded stores of William Cowan, a wholesale wine and spirit merchant who had premises in nearby Church Lane. But by 1887, Thomas Conlan had acquired the corner site and was running a bar in the building that remains the Kitchen's home today. Michael Conlan took charge of the bar in 1910 and he was succeeded by James Conlan in the 1930s. The pub remained in the Conlan family until it was sold in 1991 to James Catney, whose son Pat is the current proprietor.

For much of its long history, The Kitchen Bar has been closely linked with its neighbour, the Empire Music Hall, which over the years has provided a stage for many legendary performers, including Laurel and Hardy, Charlie Chaplin, George Formby, Lily Langtry, Will Fyffe, and Flanagan and Allen. In 1937 the first radio broadcast from a theatre stage in Ireland took place at the Empire, and shortly before it closed in 1961, the music hall was the venue for the ground-breaking production of Sam Thompson's shipyard play, *Over the Bridge*, which began its difficult journey from page to stage in another Belfast pub, THE ELBOW ROOM.

It was commonplace for the performers from these shows to nip across Telfair's Entry – now Telfair Street – during the interval or after the curtain came down for a nightcap in the Kitchen, and the bar has many mementoes of its illustrious visitors. Like its long-gone neighbour, however, the Kitchen Bar is now facing an uncertain future of its own, following the announcement of ambitious plans to redevelop Victoria Square.

THE KLONDYKE BAR | *53–55 Sandy Row*

Eulogised by photographer Bill Kirk in a book of unique pictures published in 1975, the Klondyke Bar was located in buildings dating back to at least 1870, when they were occupied by W. Priestly, whose grocery, bakery and spirit dealer's premises sat on the corner of Tea Lane opposite the Belfast and Ulster Brewing Company Ltd. According to Kirk, the bar was named after the famous Canadian gold rush of 1897 by a German immigrant who arrived in Belfast in 1906. Using whatever profits he made from his gold digging exploits, the unnamed German converted a spirit grocers on the site into a full public house. His tenure seems to have been short lived, however, for there was a new owner just four years later. Robert Wasson ran the bar from 1910 until 1938 and was succeeded by Samuel Brown Evans, who was licensee of the Klondyke until it was bought by the Housing Executive for a redevelopment scheme in 1973.

The name of the Klondyke Bar and its gold rush associations may have had a particular resonance for some of the older residents of Sandy Row, for there was at one time a belief among the folk who lived in that particular area of the city that a cache of Viking gold was hidden somewhere on Cave Hill. The Reverend W. O'Hanlon says in his 1853 book, *Walks Among the Poor of Belfast*, that some Sandy Row residents had claimed to have found the gold, but were overcome by a spell which brought darkness and confusion and caused them to leave empty-handed. The clergyman concluded: 'Sandy Row-ites are at present searching for the seventh son of a seventh son, gifted with second sight, and possessing the power to take off the spell which has for ages rested on the gold. Some of these nights the Danish gold will be dragged down to Sandy Row to make the fortune of all who are in the secret.'

LAVERY'S GIN PALACE | *12–16 Bradbury Place*

In mid-19th-century Belfast, May's Market was a boisterous marketplace where flax and fruit, eggs and butter, fowl and meat were traded vigorously between country suppliers and city buyers. The May Street market had been packing in the crowds since it opened in 1813 and it wasn't long before the presence of so many potential customers began to draw a large number of publicans to the area. One of these licensees was a William Balmer, who owned the bar closest to the market stalls on the corner of Verner Street, a thoroughfare which has since been lost to redevelopment. In 1875 he sold his bar, and the purchaser was one Thomas Lavery, a publican from Dromara, Co. Down.

The purchase was something of a gamble, for by this time the heyday of the market had passed, yet May Street was still packed with public houses. Next door to Lavery's bar was the licensed premises of Samuel Patterson, and two doors away from him was another pub owned by J. Doherty. In the next block, stretching from Market Street to Cromac Street, three out of the five business premises were spirit dealers, all hoping to make a living from the declining market crowds.

Thomas Lavery's gamble seems to have paid off, however, and in the years that followed the Lavery family was able to buy or open a number of other bars in the city. They soon owned premises at Mountpottinger, Chichester Street, the Markets, Bruce Street and the Lisburn Road, and were also the proprietors of the old ELBOW ROOM on the Dublin Road. During the latter years of the First World War, the Laverys bought a bar in Bradbury Place that had previously been owned by the Kinahan brothers and before that had been occupied by a spirit dealer called W. Rosbotham.

In the 85 years that Lavery's has been in Bradbury Place, the bar has developed into something of a Belfast institution. Its public bar attracts a wide clientele and has always been popular with students, while the poets Louis MacNeice and John Hewitt could at one time be found deep in discussion in the Cobbles, a back bar accessed from Albion Lane. Lavery's was also reputed to be one of the first pubs in the city to provide a lounge bar, a momentous move recalled by Pat Lavery in an interview he gave in 1981. 'We got a lounge so that women could come in for a drink,' said Pat, who served his apprenticeship in the bar trade in the 1930s. 'Before that, if a woman came into the public bar she would be stared at until she left. But times have changed – women are free to come into bars now and enjoy a drink just like the men.'

LENNON'S TAVERN | *Cromac Street*

This long-disappeared pub was the venue for the formation of an early Belfast branch of Daniel O'Connell's Catholic Association in 1824. The Association was founded the previous year to campaign for the right of Catholics to sit in parliament and hold state and judicial posts. It was funded by a levy of one penny per month on all its members and the sum raised in Ireland as a whole totalled £1,000 per week in 1825. After the passing of the Catholic Emancipation Act in 1829, the association dissolved since its aim had been achieved. Little is known about the exact location of Lennon's Tavern and no trace of it remains today.

THE LIFEBOAT BAR | *39–43 Queen's Square*

The sign outside this dockland pub might say that it was established in 1921, but licensed premises have existed here for much longer. The site of the Lifeboat Bar was occupied by Burn's Commercial Hotel in the 1860s, which was run by George

Parker in later years. In 1892, John Ward ran a bar at 39 Queen's Square, while the adjoining premises included the firemen and sailors' union headquarters and the offices of W. H. Malcolm, coal merchant and shipping agent.

The Lifeboat Bar went through a succession of owners' hands in the late 1930s. In 1936 it was owned by James Dolan, who passed it on to John McHugh in 1938, who in turn sold it to W. J. Quinn in 1942. In the 1960s and 1970s, the bar was owned by the McHugh family.

THE LIVERPOOL BAR | *44 Donegall Quay*

Situated just a stone's throw from the Liverpool ferry terminal, this unpretentious dockside pub was a handy refreshment stop for dock workers, cross-channel truckers and ferry passengers. The no-frills interior included a number of lifebelts from old ferryboats on the walls and in its final years the Liverpool Bar was well known for its traditional music nights.

The first known bar on this site was called the Belfast Arms, and in the late 1860s it was owned by a man named James Carlisle. By the end of the 19th century, Donegall Quay was packed with pubs catering for thirsty dock workers and sailors. At the very start of the street between the corner of Ann Street and Tedford's sailmakers, there were three pubs sandwiched together: Fullen's at No 1, Hugh Gillen's at Nos 2 and 3, and Samuel Mahood's at No 4.

In 1936 the pub at 44 Donegall Quay – located between the Missions to Seamen Institute and Coast Lines Ltd steamship company – was owned by Patrick McGeeney, who had previously been the proprietor of premises at 22 Dock Street, later to become PAT'S BAR, and was also the owner of THE CROWN and The Adelphi in Great Victoria Street. McGeeney, who owned a total of four bars in Belfast in 1942, sold the Donegall Quay bar to John Donnelly in 1947.

After being badly damaged in a bomb attack in the 1970s, the Liverpool reopened for business and carried on serving until 2000, when it was demolished to make way for a car park. The Kelly family, former owners of Kelly's Wine Stores in Short Strand, were the owners of the Liverpool Bar for many years before its eventual closure.

THE LONG BAR | *118 Leeson Street*

As its name suggests, this was a long, narrow bar with entrances from two different streets. Built in the latter half of the 19th century, the Long Bar's most famous owner was a Co Roscommon man, John Leneghan, who was the father of Mary McAleese, the first President of Ireland born in Ulster. At the outbreak of the Troubles in 1969, the rooms above the Long Bar were for a time the offices of the Catholic Citizen's Defence Committee, and for a couple of months they were also home to a pirate radio station, Radio Free Belfast, which was set up to provide an alternative information service for isolated Catholic communities during a period of sustained street violence.

Local residents outside The Long Bar in the mid-1960s

There was also a Long Bar located at 138 Shankill Road, housed beneath a boxing club, which was the training ground for many successful local boxers of the 1950s and 1960s. Both Long Bars have been lost to redevelopment.

McCAVANA'S BAR | *170 Grosvenor Road*

This establishment, which at one time stood on the corner of Distillery Street, was an old wood-panelled bar lined with snugs. One distinctive feature of the premises was a brass statue of a leprechaun smoking a pipe, which emitted a perpetual gas flame used by customers to light their cigarettes and pipes.

The owner of the bar was Edward McCavana, a Justice of the Peace and a recipient of the MBE, one of a special breed of publicans who were known to lend a discreet helping hand to needy folk in the community. If a local family was unable to meet the expense of a funeral or was hard-pressed by the arrival of a new baby, Edward McCavana would have quietly slipped them the necessary cash and was in no hurry to be reimbursed. He wasn't alone in his philanthropy either. Other Belfast publicans well known for this reputation included Sean McKeown, whose bar on the Falls Road was nicknamed 'The Decent Man' as a tribute to his generosity, and Barney Conway, proprietor of THE SPORTSMANS' ARMS in York Street.

McENANEY'S BAR | *1 Glen Road*

Dubbed the Gravedigger's Arms by local people because of its proximity to Milltown Cemetery, this Falls bar was founded in 1888 as a spirit grocers called the Brewery Stores. The McEnaney family's ownership of the premises began in 1905 with the purchase of the spirit grocers by Edward McEnaney and it continued until the early 1970s when Miss Rita McEnaney sold it to Paddy Cullen.

McENTEE'S BAR | *King Street*

Sean McEntee, one of the founder members of Fianna Fáil and a veteran of the Easter Rising in Dublin, was the most famous member of this Belfast pub-owning family. In the 1890s, the McEntees owned several bars in the city, including the MORNING STAR in Pottinger's Entry, a pub at the corner of King Street and King Street Place, another at the corner of Mill Street and a bar at 45–49 King Street.

After the 1916 Dublin rising was quelled, Sean McEntee was initially sentenced to death for his part in the insurrection, but this was later commuted to life imprisonment and he was released from prison following the general amnesty of 1917. A year later he embarked on a political career and in 1918 was elected Member of Parliament for Monaghan. During the election campaign it is said that Countess Markievicz – the first woman elected to the House of Commons, although she didn't take her seat – was a visitor to one of McEntee's bars in Belfast. Sean McEntee went on to hold ministerial posts in the Irish Government and died in 1984.

McGLADE'S | *96 Donegall Street and 31 Little Donegall Street*

Stretching some 100 feet from a location almost opposite the *Irish News* office to the rear of the *Belfast Telegraph*, P. and F. McGlade's was not only a convenient haunt for journalists, it also laid claim to being one of the longest bars in the British Isles. The downstairs 'Long Bar', at 57 feet the longest undivided bar counter in the country, was ostensibly for men only – a tradition that was eventually challenged in the courts by a prominent women's rights campaigner in 1979. Then there were the lounges, the Theatre Lounge, the Old Vic and the Penny-Farthing – space was not something that the McGlades ever had to worry about.

The McGlade family's connection with the licensed trade stretches back to the middle of the 19th century. Brothers Patrick and Frank McGlade were already the owners of a number of bars and spirit dealers in the city – among them the HERCULES BAR in Castle Street – when they took possession of premises in Donegall Street in 1888 and initially named them the Arcade. Within ten years, the brothers had monopolised the licensed premises at the junction of Donegall Street and York Street, owning the International Restaurant, Bars and Billiard Hall (which was later destroyed in the 1941 Blitz) on one corner, and the Grand Metropole Hotel on the opposite corner. By the outbreak of the First World War, however, both these premises had been sold by the brothers. When Patrick's son,

Frank, entered the trade in the 1920s the family's holdings included the Tower Buildings in Peter's Hill, the Arcade bar and billiard rooms in Donegall Street, the Queen's Cafe (a licensed restaurant in Queen's Arcade) and the Bambridge Hotel in Sugar House Entry – famous in the 1790s as PEGGY BARCLAY'S TAVERN.

Pioneers of the pub food trade, they were selling pub lunches in the 1930s, when a three-course dinner could be bought on their premises for one shilling and fourpence. When the Second World War broke out and American GIs flooded into Northern Ireland in 1942, Frank McGlade was often forced to call on his training as a boxer when rows broke out between black and white soldiers in the bar. The immaculately dressed Frank even kept a punchbag in an upstairs room that later became a lounge bar, so that he could stay in shape.

One of the more significant features of McGlade's bar was an old penny-farthing bicycle, unearthed in the loft of the building when the Old Vic lounge was being created. The Old Vic lounge earned its name from the fact that the building next door to McGlade's was formerly a theatre and the lounge itself had once been a dressing room for the performers. The old penny-farthing was said to have belonged to Patrick McGlade, who had used it to cycle to work on occasions. It was incorporated into a decorative mural designed for the Old Vic lounge by John Hunter, head of the art department at Everton Secondary School.

For a time the bicycle was also used to advertise McGlade's own brands of whiskey. One of these, called Old Bena Malt, sold for nine shillings and ninepence per bottle in the 1930s. In common with many other bars, McGlade's also bottled their own stout; a tradition that continued until 1973, when John Hannon, who had been carrying out this task at McGlade's for 38 years, finally filled his last bottle.

The year 1979 brought more changes to the bar. Green beer, a novelty at the time, was introduced on St Patrick's Day, and the bar's old ringing cash register was finally replaced with a modern electronic one.

Outside the bar, the times were changing too. The Troubles visited destruction on McGlade's in 1971, three times in 1972, three times in 1973, and again in 1974 and 1976. The only silver lining to the cloud was the fact that the bar proved a popular rendezvous for local and foreign journalists who came to Belfast to cover the events. In one year alone, more than 1,100 reporters and photographers signed the pub's visitors' book.

In September 1983, however, a fire gutted the premises, and one of the few things to be saved was Patrick McGlade's old penny-farthing bicycle. The pub had been sold to Bass Ireland about a year earlier and after the fire they demolished the building and built a new bar, which they called the Penny-Farthing. The premises have been sold a couple of times since and are now known as the Kremlin.

THE McGRATH TAVERN | *May Street*

Master McGrath was probably the most famous greyhound ever and this corner pub, which was a grocer's shop until 1850, was not simply named as a tribute to the legendary dog's exploits, but claimed a much stronger connection.

Master McGrath was the pet of a young Waterford lad named McGrath until a trainer spotted his potential and in 1867 sent him to Lord Lurgan, a prominent hare-coursing enthusiast. Within a year the greyhound had triumphed in the most celebrated coursing event of its time, the Waterloo Cup. He repeated the success in 1869, but during competition for the cup on the following year he crashed through the ice of a frozen river and almost died. The dog was nursed back to health and despite being over six years old at the time, he won the Waterloo Cup for an unprecedented third time in 1871. Such was the dog's fame after this achievement that a popular ballad was written about him and he was presented to Queen Victoria, 'where he was petted and made much of by the Royal Family'. When Master McGrath eventually died two years later, he was buried in a specially-made oak coffin, and greyhounds formed a guard of honour.

As Lord Lurgan and Master McGrath were journeying to Liverpool for their record-breaking third Waterloo Cup win, it is said they spent a night at the tavern in May Street. To mark the visit the tavern was renamed in the dog's honour and staff planted a commemorative ash tree in the back yard. The tree could still be seen in the 1940s, and although both tree and tavern are now long gone, the name of Master McGrath still has the power to stir emotions.

McHUGH'S | *29–31 Queen's Square*

When Queen Victoria paid a visit to Belfast in 1849, an area around the docks was being tidied up and laid out as a square, so the city fathers deemed it appropriate to mark the occasion by naming the new street Queen's Square in honour of her visit. Along one side of this square was a row of buildings that is believed to have predated the redevelopment by some 140 years and it's here that the forerunners of McHugh's Bar can be found.

It is difficult to be certain when a tavern was first located at this address, and the claim that the building in which it was housed dates from 1710 has been a matter for some debate. There's no doubt, however, that a bar was dispensing drink at this location by the early 19th century, and records dating from 1850 reveal that a woman named Ann Quinn was the licensee at 31 Queen's Square. Ann was certainly a busy woman, for she also ran the Queen's Square Coffee House and her premises acted as offices for the Belfast, Bangor, Newtownards and Portaferry mail car service. In 1892 Mary McConnell ran a temperance hotel at No 29 while No 31 was the public house of M. and F. Quinn.

The Quinns retained ownership until 1920 when the premises were purchased by W. J. Hendron, who some years later became the proprietor of a bar at 44 Church Lane, now known as THE ROOST. Called simply Hendron's Bar, the pub at 31 Queen's Square was managed for a period of around 25 years by the father of former West Belfast MP, Dr Joe Hendron. 'The pub was owned by my uncle, William Hendron,' the MP explained many years later. 'My father owned the Savoy Bar in Ann Street but during the slump in the 1930s he had to sell it at a great loss. He moved into this pub and ran it for my uncle. My brother Jim and I were both born here and the family lived upstairs.'

McHugh's in the Docks area – the building dates from the early 18th century

Pat McHugh, the owner who gave the bar its current and longest-standing name, ran the premises until 1996 when it was sold to Belfast pub entrepreneur James Mooney, whose Botanic Inns Ltd owns a number of premises, including The Apartment, THE BOTANIC INN, The Fly, Madison's, THE NORTHERN WHIG and THE ROTTERDAM. McHugh's closed for around eighteen months before work began on a renovation project costing more than £1 million. When the new-look premises opened in 1998, the original façade of the building was largely retained, along with a listed staircase, and the new enlarged premises had also absorbed DUBARRY'S BAR, which was just around the corner in Princes Street. The aim, said James Mooney at the time, was to turn it into 'a pub museum devoted to the history of the area, offering live entertainment and food and drink on three floors'.

McKEAG'S   *50–52 Newtownards Road*

According to local legend, the drink served in this bar on the corner of O'Kane's Lane, opposite the Popular Cinema, was supposed to have remarkable powers of rejuvenation. The premises were bought around the end of the First World War by J. and T. McKeag and they continued to run the bar until it was sold by Thomas McKeag to James G. Hunt in 1948. One former customer who remembers McKeag's recalled that when you drank the wine served there 'you entered another world'. Another swore that he saw men go in on crutches and walk out without them. Little wonder, then, that the popular local nickname for McKeag's was the Power Station.

McSHANNON'S   *135–137 Albertbridge Road*

One of the distinguishing features about this bar, which once dominated the junction of the Albertbridge Road and Castlreagh Street, was a large stone which stood at the front of the premises, and although the pub is no longer in existence, the stone can still be seen there today.

It has been fancifully suggested that William of Orange once used the stone to mount his horse during the course of his Irish campaign, but there's no evidence to suggest that King Billy ever tied up his white charger at this spot. Others say that farmers attending local markets would have used this stone to climb onto their horses, but perhaps the most intriguing notion is that it is one of the last surviving remnants of the Long Bridge, whose 21 arches spanned the Lagan from 1688 until 1845. It's said that the stone was rescued by a local builder, Francis Ritchie, who had the job of knocking down the Long Bridge and replacing it with the Queen's Bridge. Ritchie presented this souvenir of a long-established Belfast landmark to a local doctor, who promptly placed it in his garden and unwittingly created a new landmark in the east of the city.

The first premises at this location to serve drink was probably the grocery and spirit dealer's business of Archibald Blaney, which was founded in the 1860s. By 1910 James McShannon, who lived on the nearby Newtownards Road, had taken possession of the premises and it remained in the family for 60 years. In the early 1970s, new owners renamed it Clancy's Tavern and it survived until the late 1980s.

MADDEN'S BAR   *Berry Street*

The area around Smithfield has changed enormously since the massive Castlecourt shopping centre cut a swathe through the area in 1990. Before that Madden's Bar, whose former address was 74 Smithfield, was part of the bustling honeycomb of streets where shops and stalls were packed tightly together and the pubs were thronged with shoppers and traders. Today, however, the concrete and glass wedge of Castlecourt divides Madden's from its former hinterland.

Berry Street too has changed almost beyond recognition. If you had strolled down this street in the year 1850 you would have found it peppered with second-

Madden's Bar tucked away in the former Smithfield Markets area

hand clothes shops from end to end. Of the 41 premises occupying Berry Street in that year, 32 of them were clothes dealers, trading so briskly that they had to import second-hand clothes from Scotland. Of the remaining nine buildings, two of them were pubs – Peter McGouran's spirit store at No 1 and John Crawford Jr, grocer and spirit dealer, at No 25. As a counterbalance to the lure of drink and mammon, Berry Street was also home to a Teetotal Hall and a Presbyterian Meeting House.

According to the sign above the door of the present bar, Madden's had already been in existence for over a century by this time. It is claimed that the pub has been serving drink in the Smithfield area since 1751, but it wasn't until the 1870s that the first Madden took over the premises from a spirit dealer named James Bogan. Michael Madden was the first of the family to own the bar at 74 Smithfield, and from then on the *Belfast Street Directory* variously describes the owner as Mrs Madden (from the turn of the century until the 1930s), Miss B. J. Madden (from the mid-1930s until the 1960s) and from the 1960s onwards it is simply listed as Madden's Bar.

Despite all the changes that have taken place, the bar remains a popular spot and has become well known for its traditional music sessions, both organised and spontaneous. But if it's second-hand clothes you're looking for, you'll be sorely disappointed by Berry Street today.

THE MARITIME HOTEL | 36 College Square North

Hub of the blues boom in Belfast during the 1960s, this former Royal Irish Constabulary (RIC) barracks built at the turn of the century became famous as the venue that launched the careers of Van Morrison and Them. After the RIC no longer needed the building it was converted into a mission house for seamen, which played host to a rhythm and blues club on Friday nights to attract students and young people. Van Morrison and Them made their first appearance at the Maritime on 17 April 1964. Them's guitarist Billy Harrison recalled: 'The three Js – Jerry, Jerry and Jimmy – took over the Maritime Hotel, a trad jazz gig in College Square North, and approached us to play blues there. The first time we played the Maritime there were 50 people, the second night 180; the third night we sold out – and we sold out as long as Them were there.' Van Morrison is quoted as saying that Them 'lived and died as a group on the stage at the Maritime Hotel'. The hotel was demolished around 1991.

THE MERMAID INN | 5–7 Wilson's Court

Located in the very heart of old Belfast, just yards from where sailing ships would have docked alongside the quays of High Street, the Mermaid is one of the few survivors of a time when the narrow laneways leading off High Street would have been crammed with inns and hotels serving sailors, travellers, merchants and dock workers. The Mermaid is said to be around 200 years old and was known as George Johnston's Rainbow Hotel around the middle of the 19th century. Before that, the premises were known as the Harp Tavern and were run by a publican named John Sheals. Also in Wilson's Court in the early 1800s was another well-known inn, Gillett's, while Maria McNabb operated a tavern at 14 Wilson's Court in 1819. A couple of decades earlier the little laneway had earned some notoriety as the home of the *Northern Star*, newspaper of the United Irishmen and a thorn in the side of officialdom.

During the early 1930s, the Mermaid was owned by a Mrs A. Hamilton, who sold it to John Magowan in 1937. He in turn accepted an offer for the pub from Mrs Annie Armstrong in 1942 and there have been many owners since. The sailing ships, the dockside merchants and the *Northern Star* may have long since disappeared into history but take a stroll up old Wilson's Court today and you'll still find the Mermaid serving away.

MOLLY WARD'S TAVERN | *Stranmillis*

In the late 18th century, Molly Ward's was not only a popular destination for the fashionable folk of Belfast but was also one of the favourite meeting places of the United Irishmen. It's said that Wolfe Tone, Henry Joy McCracken, Samuel Neilson and Thomas Russell were all frequent visitors to the tavern beside the Lagan lock-gates. In his collection of historical sketches, *As I Roved Out*, writer Cathal O'Byrne says that during the years leading up to the 1798 rebellion, arms and gun-powder were taken off ships anchored in Belfast Lough and carried in small boats up the Lagan to be stored in Molly Ward's Tavern. However, when an informant told the authorities about the cache, most of it was either quickly dispersed or thrown into the Lagan. The yeomanry searched the tavern thoroughly but found nothing – a barrel of gunpowder that was discovered by Molly at the last minute was hidden from the searching soldiers by persuading her aged mother-in-law to sit on it! Frustrated by his lack of success, the commanding officer withdrew Molly's drinks licence, and the tavern's days as a fashionable watering hole were brought to an abrupt end.

THE MONICO | *17 Lombard Street*

Just around the corner from one of the city's oldest bars, WHITE'S TAVERN, the Monico shares a similar, if shorter, heritage with White's in that it too was once a wine and spirit merchants. Although the building has been associated with the drinks trade since 1880, it didn't become known as the Monico until 1901. In the 1890s it was the premises of Boucher and Thomson, family grocers and wine and spirit merchants. Purchased by the Lynch family in the mid-1930s – Thaddeus Lynch also owned a pub at Carlisle Circus – the Monico's main bar is reassuringly traditional in style, with a tiled floor, wood panelling, solid counter and five open snugs. The small lounge at the rear opens on to the mural-decorated courtyard of Winecellar Entry. The bar was purchased from solicitor Edward Lynch by the Diver family, which also currently owns WHITE'S TAVERN.

MOONEY'S | *1–3 Arthur Square*

Up until about 1980, Mooney's Bar, with its granite-topped counter and decorative tiling, was a popular city centre rendezvous for drinkers and diners. It had been acquired in 1897 by the well-known Dublin firm of J. G. Mooney and Co, but had been a hostelry and eating establishment for perhaps 50 years before that. The site was formerly a provision store built by Alex Moreland in 1825, and then it became the Thistle Hotel, which survived until around 1890.

The building was refurbished at a cost of £8,000 and reopened as the Grand Restaurant, but despite all the money that was lavished upon it, the Grand Restaurant didn't last, and a short time later the premises came into the posses-sion of James Moir. He had ambitious plans for the place, and produced a menu offering bird's nest soup, Bombay duck and bear's ham – whatever that might have

Mooney's – a bustling spot in 1930s Belfast (from the Hogg Collection, Ulster Museum)

been. Perhaps his plans were just too ambitious for turn-of-the-century Belfast, for Moir soon went the way of his predecessors.

Culinary innovation continued when J. G. Mooney took it over in 1897, for the upstairs was given over to the XL Vegetarian Restaurant, no doubt a rarity in late Victorian Belfast. In the 1960s and 1970s, when Mooney's bar manager was Barney Mulvey, you could buy a 'Barney Special', which was chopped ham and chicken with mushrooms, coated with a cream sauce and topped with asparagus. Hardly Bombay duck or bird's nest soup, but the lunchtime crowds loved it.

Down this narrow thoroughfare connecting High Street and Ann Street you could, at one time, have had your pick of bars. In the mid-1800s you might have been tempted by the Eagle Tavern or the Pottinger Arms Hotel, while not quite a century later you might have stepped into the Hemisphere Bar for a glass or two. The Morning Star, however, has outlasted them all.

No one knows exactly how long The Morning Star has been there, although the building it occupies seems to date back to the early 19th century. It has been

The etched glass windows of The Morning Star help make it one of Belfast's visual delights

claimed that the bar was mentioned in the *Belfast News-Letter* of 1810, although others suggest the bar was built in 1820 and was known as the Scotch Oyster House in the mid-1800s. In 1892, two publicans called McEntee and McKenna, who at the time owned a couple of pubs in the Castle Street area, were the proprietors of a bar at this location in Pottinger's Entry. By the end of the century, however, the partnership seems to have dissolved and the premises became known as H. McKenna's bottling store and wine merchants. Mr McKenna remained the proprietor for at least another 20 years and it was during his ownership, in 1913, that the pub was first listed in the *Belfast Street Directory* as the Morning Star Luncheon Bar.

Whatever the truth of its history, the Morning Star is undoubtedly one of Belfast's gems. The bar is immediately recognisable by its fine glass and wrought iron sign, topped by a wine jug that lost one of its handles during the Troubles – since replaced. Guarding the door at the corner is a startling sculpture of the winged lion of St Mark.

The ground floor interior is dominated by a horseshoe bar, installed in 1925 when the Morning Star underwent extensive reconstruction. The work was undertaken by the new owners of the bar, James and Edward Madden, who at that time also owned the Ivy Bar in Church Lane, the Dufferin House in Whitla Street, the SPORTSMAN'S ARMS in York Street and a spirit store in Duncairn Gardens. A newspaper announcement from the time declared that 'the new proprietors are resolved that for quick service, good viands and fine liquors, the house shall rank second to none in the city. Its central situation makes it a convenient resort for the busy business man whose luncheon interval is often cut short'.

MULDOON'S | *13 Corporation Square*

For centuries this area has been at the very hub of Belfast's nautical industry. In the late 18th century a Scotsman named William Ritchie established Belfast's first shipbuilding company here and for many years afterwards the street was known as Ritchie's Dock. Alongside the elegant Harbour Offices and Sinclair Seamen's Presbyterian Church, a succession of bonded warehouses, steamship offices, chandleries and rope makers have come and gone in Corporation Square, and so too have the street's many hotels and taverns. At one time the square offered a wide range of accommodation for seamen; Mrs Potter's Marine Hotel and Tavern, popular in the middle of the 19th century, being an example.

Around 1860 a tavern was established by Thomas Wilson at the corner of Corporation Square and Tomb Street. In 1899 it was owned by P. Flynn, while the Marine Hotel next door had become Miss Long's Pilot Hotel and Samuel McAuley had a bar on the opposite corner of Tomb Street. The McConville family took possession of the bar at No 13 around 1910, seven years later it was bought by a Mrs W. J. Purdy, and then in 1921 the name above the door changed to that of J. and W. Muldoon. The bar remains a popular dockside hostelry today.

THE NORTHERN WHIG | *2 Bridge Street*

While the Northern Whig bar is one of the city's newest, it is by no means the first licensed premises to be located here. This spot at one of the oldest parts of Belfast called the Four Corners – where Rosemary Street, North Street, Bridge Street and Waring Street meet – was formerly occupied by a row of four thatched cottages in the turbulent 1790s. The third cottage in this row housed a tiny bar called the Thatched House Tavern, which was used as a regular meeting place for the Presbyterian-led republican society, the United Irishmen.

The tavern was a particularly convenient location for one of the founders of the United Irishmen, Samuel Neilson, for the cottage next door to the little pub

The Northern Whig, situated at The Four Corners – one of the oldest parts of Belfast. The building was partially destroyed in the 1941 air attacks and the area became known as 'Blitz Square'.

was occupied by Neilson's drapery shop. (The cottage on the other side was a grocery shop owned by Valentine Jones, who also ran a wine merchants in Winecellar Entry on the site of what is now WHITE'S TAVERN.)

In 1822, the thatched cottages were torn down to make way for Commercial Buildings, a multi-purpose venue, which included a hotel among its facilities and served for 13 years as the Town Hall. The Commercial Hotel, which provided a terminus for the Dublin coach was initially run by a Mrs Faloon and in the 1840s was taken over by Peter Echlin. At the turn of the century, a Mr R. B. Hall was in charge.

Around 1922, Commercial Buildings became the home of the *Northern Whig* newspaper, which had been founded almost a century earlier by Francis Dalzell Finlay with the lofty aim of providing 'a Press that no man shall call servant, and that will acknowledge no master but the Law'. The willing champion of a brand of liberal unionism that had previously been the preserve of the *Belfast News-Letter*, the *Northern Whig* became a daily in 1858 after first being published weekly and then three times a week. The final edition of the *Northern Whig* was published in 1963.

PAT'S BAR | *19–22 Princes Dock Street*

It is only in recent years that a solitary pub has been located at this address at the end of Princes Dock Street. For over a century it was two bars, one at Nos 19–20 and the other at Nos 21–22. In 1870, the first bar was William Dempsey's and the second was John McAlister's Seaview Tavern. By 1892, John Marnell and John Boal were the neighbouring publicans.

Two of the longest-serving landlords at these addresses were Sheila Maguire, who bought Nos 19–20 in 1934 and ran the place for 30 years, and Lawrence Meeghan, who also became a proprietor in the mid-1930s and continued until the 1960s. Barney's Bar, named after the landlord Bernard McMahon, disappeared in the late 1970s and Pat's Bar, owned by P. J. Brennan and Sons – who for a time also owned THE GREAT EASTERN on the Newtownards Road – eventually spread into both premises.

Today this area of the dockland is much changed, with modern apartments, espresso bars and high-tech businesses dotted among the warehouses and chandleries. Pat's Bar now has entrances from Princes Dock Street and Barrow Square, an attractive area with picnic tables and ornamental planting. However, the sign above the door, proclaiming the bar's foundation in 1863, confirms that this particular corner of the dockland dates from a time when the surroundings were very different indeed.

PEGGY BARCLAY'S TAVERN | *2 Sugar House Entry*

When the *Luftwaffe* dropped almost 96,000 incendiary bombs on Belfast during the night of 4 May 1941, the casualties from the resulting firestorm included 150 people killed, the shipyards devastated and a significant piece of the city's history wiped out forever. The historical casualty was Peggy Barclay's Tavern, which 150 years earlier had been one of the favourite meeting places of the Society of United Irishmen as they plotted the Rebellion of 1798. Sugar House Entry, which connected High Street and Waring Street and was named after the sugar-refining industry that had been carried on there since 1704, was obliterated from the map of Belfast, never to be rebuilt. Fittingly, one end of the lane is now the site of the Northern Ireland War Memorial Building.

Down this narrow entry, Peggy Barclay's Tavern was marked by a hanging sign featuring a portrait of Benajmin Franklin, the scientist and statesman who helped to draft the American Declaration of Independence. The inn was often known as the Dr Franklin Tavern, and although it appears that Peggy Barclay was the proprietor for just a few short years following the death of her husband James, she seems to have made quite an impression on her clientele. 'What a house was Peggy's in the Entry,' wrote one customer. '"Doctor Franklin", awful and pompous, stood in a swinging frame over the door, telling all visitors, in my humble opinion, to eat, drink, and be merry, which they did, for there was plenty of accommodation for all who came. Some 20 or 30 rooms supplied the necessary space; the fertile oyster beds of Carrick and Comber supplied the dainties; and in all Ireland there was no better rum to be found than that hidden in Peggy's cellar.'

The tavern is said to have provided a discreet rendezvous for the United Irishmen during the early 1790s, and their meetings were often held in an upstairs room under the cover name of the Muddler's Club (see also THE CROWN TAVERN). 'The ostensible business was jovial amusement,' wrote one of the 'club' members, 'its real one extending the connection of the Society of United Irishmen, and it was visited by every man of known integrity who came on business to town'.

But the Muddler's Club was short-lived. It was broken up in 1796 after an employee at the tavern named Belle Martin betrayed the insurgents to the authorities. Four members named by Belle Martin were hanged at Lisburn on 18 May 1797. As a result of its association with the United Irishmen, Peggy Barclay's Tavern became a target for official harassment. Soldiers attacked and damaged the sign of Dr Franklin above the door and the story goes that Peggy was hounded out of business by vengeful officialdom. She sold up to a man named Tibbold Haycock, and later owners included William Faloon and a Mr J. Prey.

In 1839, Abraham Bambridge bought the tavern and ran it for the next 30 years. Although it had a number of other owners after that, including Patrick and Frank McGlade who later ran McGLADE'S BAR in Donegall Street, it was still called Bambridge's Hotel on the night the *Luftwaffe* reduced it to ashes.

As for Peggy Barclay, it seems that she didn't completely abandon the licensed trade when she left Sugar House Entry. Undaunted, she bought premises at Buttermilk Loaning (now Skegoneill Avenue) and gave them the unlikely name of the 'Mill for Grinding Old People Young'. The sign above the inn door showed a line of old folk hobbling into a mill building, only to emerge rejuvenated and sprightly on the other side. In keeping with her new health-giving image, Peggy's most popular drink was not the finest rum in Ireland, but milk.

THE PHOENIX BAR | *179-181 Antrim Road*

In early 1946 this distinctive Antrim Road bar was the scene of one of the most amazing accidents ever seen on the streets of Belfast. The story begins one February morning at the Cliftonville tram terminus, around a mile away from the Phoenix, where three women and two children aged four and two were sitting aboard a tram as it began to trundle slowly on its way. It was only when the tramcar gathered more speed than seemed normal that the passengers realised there was no driver or conductor on board.

Seeing the runaway tram begin to career down the sloping street, the driver and conductor ran after it, but they quickly realised they were not going to catch up with it and commandeered a lorry to give chase. As the passengers searched frantically for a way to stop the tearaway trolleybus the lorry containing the driver and conductor drew alongside. They tried to shout instructions to a woman in the driver's cab, but she couldn't hear them above the terrible din. Fearing for her life but still clutching her bag of groceries, the woman then astounded onlookers by leaping from the speeding tram. Provisions scattered everywhere as the woman hit the road, and although she was badly bruised and shocked by her leap to safety, fortunately the only casualties were her watch and spectacles.

Meanwhile the tram, with its remaining passengers still on board, sped on. 'The trolley was shaken off the overhead wires about halfway down the straight and waved violently from side to side,' reported the *Belfast Telegraph*. 'Finally, the vehicle reached its highest speed down the hill past Belfast Royal Academy and at the bottom left the rails and plunged across the Antrim Road.'

The tram was eventually halted by the gable end of the Phoenix Bar, and although the pub suffered some minor damage it was Lorenzo Turner's bootmaker's shop next door that bore the brunt of the impact. His premises were almost completely destroyed and the bootmaker and his assistant only narrowly escaped serious injury. The remaining tram passengers were also remarkably unhurt.

At the time of the accident, the Phoenix Bar was already firmly established as a popular Antrim Road watering hole. It was founded in the latter half of the 19th century and was owned for many years by a wine and spirit merchant called James Fleming. In the early 1900s Fleming entered into a partnership with a man named Lindsay and the duo were still running the bar when it famously acted as a buffer for the runaway tram in 1946.

The Antrim Road bar wasn't the only notable Belfast pub called the Phoenix, however. Another one with the same name was a popular haunt in Millfield for many years. Nicknamed the 'Fly House', the Phoenix in Millfield was said to be something of a rough spot. One former customer recalls the sound of sizzling spittle as the regulars used a pot-bellied stove in the middle of the bar as a makeshift spitoon!

THE PLOUGH HOTEL | *7 Corn Market*

Once known as Shambles Street because of the number of butchers and abattoirs in the area, Corn Market was also home to a number of hostelries, and the best known of these in the early 1800s was the Plough Tavern and Hotel. In 1835, the premises were owned by a George Davis and they stood adjacent to Smyth's Hotel and Tavern at No 5.

The Plough was frequented by travellers from all parts of Ireland, for in addition to serving as the terminus for the Dublin and Londonderry mail and passenger coaches, there were also daily coach connections with Armagh, Banbridge, Hillsborough, Lisburn, Portadown and Tandragee. It seems that practically anyone who travelled any distance at that time would have known the Plough intimately. As well as providing rest and refreshment for coach passengers, the hotel also featured a pioneering entertainment venue, the New Harmonic Saloon, featuring regular singers and musicians, in the early 1830s.

In 1867, the Plough was demolished and replaced by a new development, appropriately named Plough Chambers. As this new building was being completed, an enterprising firm of wine importers and distillers, W & A Gilbey, was setting up its Belfast office next door at 3 Corn Market.

The Gilbey brothers had initially established their business in London in 1857 and when they expanded into Belfast ten years later they appointed a Mr F. Guerin as manager. Probably the most curious aspect of Gilbey's Corn Market office was the unique little bar that operated just above their street level wine shop. It's unclear when this bar was first established, but it was still going in the late 1960s and possibly into the early 1970s. The best description of how to gain entry to the bar comes from a helpful guidebook of the time:

'From the pavement you can see an excellent wine shop and upon entering you will find one of the most unusual features ever met by any drinker. It is a lift with a button marked bar and to one's enjoyment, when pressed, it will take you direct to this famous establishment. Do not forget to turn at right angles when it stops in order to leave, as this can be confusing if you feel light-headed. If you wish to take a few minutes rest from the bustle of the 20th century a visit here is recommended.'

The upper floor at Gilbey's became the haunt of many local personalities and was a favourite meeting place for members of the licensed trade. However, a tightening up of fire regulations for commercial premises meant inevitable closure for a bar which could only be accessed by a lift. The site of this unusual watering hole and the old Plough Hotel up the street it is now occupied by British Home Stores.

THE POUND | *Townhall Street*

Charles McManus owned a pub in Oxford Street at the turn of the century and also had a stabling yard in nearby Townhall Street to cater for the many country folk who came to Belfast for the city's livestock markets. In the early years of the 20th century, the stabling yard was accompanied by McManus's Hotel and a photograph from around 1912 clearly shows premises known as the Pound beside the hotel. By 1920 the yard was owned by a Robert Roddy, and he passed it on to an L. Roddy, who created a café on the site in the mid-1930s. Within 20 years the café had turned into a thriving pub called the Pound, which later earned great popularity as a rock music bar in the entertainment-starved Belfast of the 1970s. By the end of that decade, however, the Pound had poured its last pint.

THE REX BAR | *215 Shankill Road*

Located on the corner of Moscow Street – one of a number of roads off the Shankill named after European capitals – this landmark bar was once owned by leading businessman Dr Billy Hastings, who in subsequent years created Northern Ireland's largest independent chain of hotels, the Hastings Hotels group.

The Hastings family pub business had been established in east Belfast by Billy's parents, William and Jessie, and by the 1930s they had bought up a number of premises across the city, including the Deramore Arms, the Primrose, the Avenue One and the Scotch Row. William died when Billy was just 12 years old and his 16-year-old brother Roy took over the running of the family's bars. Although not originally intending to join the licensed trade, Billy eventually teamed up with Roy, and the pair ran the pub chain until Roy's untimely death in 1954. Billy then assumed full control of the business, which at this time included ownership of three Shankill Road bars, the Rex, the nearby Crimea Tavern and the Mountainview Tavern beyond the graveyard. The Mountainview was another old pub, which dated back to at least 1870 and it was still part of the Hastings chain when it was destroyed by a bomb in 1971. In that same year, Billy bought the Grand Metropolitan Group of Hotels and gradually moved out of the pub business.

During his time in the licensed trade he had also founded a successful wholesale drinks business and in the 1950s – the period when the Rex became a Hastings pub – he was the first person to acquire the rights to distribute Carlsberg beer in Northern Ireland.

The Rex Bar is probably the oldest surviving licensed premises on the Shankill Road. It dates back at least to the 1860s when it was owned by a man named Hugh Irvine, who ran the bar for more than 20 years. Throughout its long life, the Rex has changed hands many times. Perhaps one of the longest-serving owners was Joseph D. Kirk, who lived at 39 Woodvale Road further up the Shankill and took possession of the bar in the 1890s. During his 30-year proprietorship, Kirk also snapped up another bar on the Shankill Road, on the corner of nearby Aberdeen Street.

Around 1928 Joseph Kirk sold out to a J. Craven and by the mid-1930s the Rex had passed into the hands of W. T. Craven. At the end of the Second World War, the bar was sold to an Edward Farwell for £4,820, but his proprietorship only lasted a year before it was sold on to Horace W. Craven – very likely a relative of the bar's previous owner – in 1947. At the same time as he purchased the Rex, Craven also snapped up a combined petrol station and pub (a business venture that surely wouldn't be allowed today) at 358 Shankill Road, near the corner of Battenberg Street. Other owners that followed included R. Robinson and the partnership of McBurney and Laverty, who also owned bars at 2 Woodvale Road and 43 Albertbridge Road.

ROBINSON'S | *38 Great Victoria Street*

For a period of almost 70 years leading up to 1914, this bustling bar was called the Dublin and Armagh Hotel, but in the months before the First World War it dropped its hotel status and became known simply as Robinson's, after its then owner William Robinson, whose ownership of the premises lasted for four decades.

Robinson's is one of Belfast's best-known bars and one of the few city centre establishments to keep the pints pouring while others shut their doors at teatime during the very darkest days of the Troubles in the 1970s. If you had called into the place for a glass or two in early 1991 you would have seen a very traditional interior – black and white tiles on the floor, an impressively solid mahogany counter and six leather-upholstered snugs facing it. But three days before St Patrick's Day in that year, practically all of it was reduced to ashes in a terrorist firebomb attack.

There was really never any question of it not being rebuilt, however. So on the site where the Dublin and Armagh Hotel had once stood, a new Robinson's was raised and reopened in late 1993 at a cost of around £2 million.

A key part of Robinson's popularity down through the years has been its location at the point where visitors streamed in and out of Belfast. Built by James Keyland in 1846, the Dublin and Armagh Hotel was the first in a row of three hotels specifically created to cater for this busy throng of travellers. Beside it was

The landmark clock on the façade of Robinson's keeps time on Great Victoria Street

the Ulster Railway Hotel, later to become the CROWN LIQUOR SALOON, and on the other side of Amelia Street was the Downshire Arms Hotel, which is now THE BEATEN DOCKET. For a period stretching from the early 20th century until the mid-1960s a fourth hotel, Miss Rogan's Temperance Hotel, was sandwiched in between the Dublin and Armagh and Ulster Railway Hotels.

James Keyland's hotel was constructed just a few years after the first passengers stepped aboard the Ulster Railway from Belfast to Lisburn and the hotel had become a natural stopoff point for travellers by the time James Watson assumed ownership in the 1860s. Later, the Great Northern Railway station in Great Victoria Street became the principal point of departure for Dublin, with the first 'Enterprise' express travelling the intercity route in 1932. The author of a 1967 guide to Belfast commented: 'It would be difficult to make even a guess at the number of visitors from Dublin and the South who over the years have made Robinson's their first call on leaving the train'.

Still later, as Great Victoria Street became a terminus for country bus routes and a boarding point for buses running to Aldergrove airport, many more travellers would pop into Robinson's for sustenance while they waited for a connection.

From the 1930s until 1970, the bar was owned by the O'Neill family – current owners of THE GARRICK in Chichester Street – and on the first floor for a time there was an O'Neill Restaurant. Then for another ten years it belonged to the Rice and Diver families. In the early 1980s, the Guinness subsidiary Croft Inns purchased the premises. Around this time, Robinson's hit the headlines over a much-publicised court case in which a BBC presenter took an action against the bar for alleged sex discrimination. The TV personality claimed he had been refused entry to an upstairs bar because he was wearing jeans while two women, also wearing jeans, had been admitted by the doormen. However, the judge declared that he could not see 'a single shred' of discrimination by the bar and dismissed the case.

Although the ground floor decor in Robinson's was very traditional in style, upstairs it was a different matter. The Robinson Crusoe lounge on the first floor was fitted out like an 18th-century sailing ship, with rigging, masthead, lanterns and all manner of nautical fixtures. The lounge was destroyed in the fire of 1991, but the penchant for themed bars carried over into the new Robinson's opened in 1993. A library effect was created on the ground floor, with life-size mannequins of Sherlock Holmes and Dr Watson, while in the back bar the theme was that of a turn-of-the-century general merchants and upstairs was styled like a prohibition-era speakeasy. It's all a far cry from the Dublin and Armagh Hotel, but even today you'll still find plenty of folk pausing in their travels to while away an hour or two in Robinson's.

THE ROCK | *491 Falls Road*

Probably the oldest surviving family-run bar in Belfast, The Rock was founded in the early 1900s by Frank O'Neill and until late 2001 a fourth generation of the O'Neill family was actively involved in the business. Before they built the Rock, the O'Neills owned Beagan's Bar on the Springfield Road and another pub in Ashmore Street, which opened its doors on Good Friday, 1888. Frank O'Neill was deeply dedicated to building up the family business and it's said that even on his wedding day he went straight back to the bar as soon as the ceremony was over.

The capital needed to build The Rock was raised from the sale of a bar on the Grosvenor Road, which was bought by the Royal Victoria Hospital as a site for the expansion of its medical facilities. At the same time as The Rock was taking shape,

Frank O'Neill inspecting the work on the new Rock Bar in 1900

Belfast's new City Hall was being built in Donegall Square, and when the City Hall stonemasons took strike action in a dispute with their employers, Frank O'Neill gave them work creating the decorative sandstone façade of his new bar.

A photograph currently hanging on the wall of the bar (shown above) shows a proud Frank O'Neill standing in front of a partially completed Rock Bar. The more observant will notice that it was originally a three-storey building, whereas today the Rock has only two storeys. The third storey was apparently destroyed in a fire which is said to have started in 1944 on the day Frank's grandson, also called

Frank, was born. At that time, the O'Neills, in common with many other bars, bottled their own stout and the corks that were no longer of any use were often thrown on the upstairs fire at the end of the day. On this particular occasion, it is believed that the large number of corks thrown on the embers caused the fire to blaze up and set a wooden roof beam alight.

This wasn't the only time The Rock suffered a fire, however. In the early 1920s, the bar was taken over by the Black and Tans and was severely damaged in an arson attack. But despite these setbacks, The Rock continued to prosper over the years and in the late 1960s the bar was expanded through the removal of an adjoining house. One thing which has not changed in all that time, however, is the distinctive exterior stonework created one hundred years ago by those striking City Hall masons.

THE ROOST | *44–46 Church Lane*

When German bombs rained down on the heart of old Belfast on the night of 4 May 1941, three pubs in Church Lane were among the thousands of buildings damaged or destroyed. Alexander McCann's Store Bar at No 21 survived the onslaught, but another McCann pub at No 31 was wrecked, as were Patrick Kelly's bar at No 36 and W. J. Hendron's bar at No 44. Hendron owned a number of other Belfast bars at the time, including a pub not far away at 100 Ann Street that has been variously known as the Lagan Bar, the Auto Inn and the Savoy Bar, and premises at Queen's Square that later became known as McHugh's.

It is said there has been a pub at 44 Church Lane since the latter half of the 18th century. In 1899 it was the premises of P. Duffy and Co, and by 1910 it was owned by P. Murray. William Hendron purchased the place in the early 1930s. The bar didn't become known as The Roost until it was reopened in 1962 by Paddy Hunt and Jack Hinds, the founders of the Irish Bonding Company, who also owned the Bar 40 in East Belfast.

THE ROTTERDAM | *54 Pilot Street*

Imagine yourself taking a stroll down Pilot Street, a bustling dockside cul-de-sac, in the year 1850. Every glance would have taken in either a tavern or some indication of Belfast's maritime industry. At No 2 there would have been dock workers tucking into great platefuls of food at Edward Glenfield's Washington Coffee and Chop Tavern, while across the road Peter Barker's pub would have been serving up foaming pints of porter. Other licensees on the street in that year included John Hogg, Robert Anderson, John Wilson and Captain James McKey, who ran the Ship Hotel and Tavern. Elsewhere there were ship smiths, sawyers, sail makers, watch and clock makers, block and pump makers, the residences of several sea captains, a master mariner and, not surprisingly, the home of a pilot, Alex Dyer. This street was undoubtedly at the heart of dockland.

It has been said that the original licence for The Rotterdam dates back to 1820, and the building in which it is housed is claimed to be 30 years older still.

The Rotterdam – a revitalised bar in the heart of Belfast's dockland

What is known for certain is that in 1870 a publican named John Crone was operating from premises at 54 Pilot Street, and from then on a tavern continued to do business at this address.

The Rotterdam name may have been inspired by a ship of that name which was built by Harland and Wolff for the Holland-America Line and launched in 1897, although there appears to be evidence to suggest that the name was attached to the premises as early as 1892, when they were owned by Mrs Alice Kelly. It's said that in former times the building was used as a holding centre for convicts before they were transported to Tasmania, and the shackles attached to the walls were supposedly visible for many years afterwards.

In 1910 The Rotterdam's proprietor was a John Crealy, who was probably related to Patrick Crealy, the owner of the nearby American Hotel on the corner of Dock Street and Short Street. The landlord in the 1920s was a P. Greeney and in 1929 it was taken over by Joseph Donnelly, whose family ran the bar successfully for a number of decades and whose name is still visible in large letters on the gable wall. By the early 1980s, however, it seemed as if The Rotterdam's days as a dockland watering hole were long gone. The building was little more than a burnt-out shell and there appeared to be little interest in restoring it – until, that is, two young entrepreneurs called Ernie Magennis and Chris Roddy decided to bring the Rotterdam back to life.

With a loan of £4,000 and a weekly payment of £40 each from the Enterprise Allowance Scheme, the pair began the challenging task of restoring the bar. 'We wanted to create a bar that was rough at the edges but full of character,' Chris told an interviewer. 'We hunted around skips and derelict buildings for the wood, which we stripped, varnished and then used for seating, and to build the counter.'

After much hard work The Rotterdam was reopened on 23 November 1984, and within a few years it had become one of the city's most popular live music venues, hosting Irish, African, blues, jazz, folk and Cajun bands. The revitalised bar was also used as the setting for a TV comedy drama written by Belfast playwright Martin Lynch.

Another of its distinctive features was the huge range of spirits stored behind the bar. It's said that the Vintners' Association once carried out a survey into the variety of brands stocked by every bar in Northern Ireland. The stocktaker spent a few hours in each one taking note of the various products sold. When he arrived at The Rotterdam, however, he was still taking notes after three days...

THE ROYAL HOTEL | *55–61 Donegall Place*

Sir Arthur Chichester, the man often credited with founding the city of Belfast, would surely have turned in his grave had he known how enthusiastically the family fortune and reputation he had worked so hard to build up would be whittled away by his descendant George Augustus, the second Marquis of Donegall. George and family had been living and spending happily in England for many years until a mounting queue of angry creditors started knocking loudly on the door. Rather than pay up – not for nothing was he known as the Marquis of Done-'em-all – George fled to Belfast. Arriving with family in tow in 1802 he set up house at the corner of Donegall Place and Donegall Square, opposite the site of what later became Robinson and Cleaver's store.

Thinking he was safe from his creditors, the intemperate marquis continued to work his way through the family fortune with a steely dedication and was soon forced to sell the city centre home he had christened Donegall House. The Donegalls moved to Ormeau and the house which bore their name was ignominiously sold to the family's former butler, Charles Kerns.

Kerns set about converting the house into a hotel and in 1824, the Royal Hotel opened its doors for business. It wasn't long before the Royal was entertaining some of Belfast's most prestigious visitors. In 1842, William Makepeace Thackeray, the author of *Vanity Fair*, booked into the hotel as he toured Ireland gathering material for his *Irish Sketch Book*.

'With respect to the inn, that in which I stayed (Kearn's) was as comfortable and well ordered an establishment as the most fastidious Cockney can desire,' he wrote, 'and with an advantage which some people, perhaps, do not care for, that the dinners which cost seven shillings at London taverns are here served for half a crown.'

More controversial was the visit of the 'Great Liberator' Daniel O'Connell in 1841. Touring the country to campaign for the repeal of the Act of Union, O'Connell arrived in Belfast at 6 pm on Saturday, 16 January, and remained in the Royal Hotel for most of the following day. 'Yesterday a sort of levee was held at

*The Royal Hotel advertised itself on its side wall facing onto Donegall Square in the late
19th century (Welch Collection, Ulster Museum)*

the hotel,' reported the *Belfast News-Letter*, 'and all visitors, including the
Hercules-street boys, were graciously received and saluted after the most
approved fashion.'

On Tuesday, 19 January, O'Connell addressed a large crowd from the balcony
of the hotel. His words met with a boisterous reception, however, and on
occasions he was drowned out by hecklers. Later on, a number of the hotel
windows were smashed.

O'Connell's residency at the Royal Hotel was followed by visits from other distinguished guests, including Charles Dickens and the opera singer Jenny Lind.

Charles Kerns eventually passed on the mantle of ownership to a Miss Sarah Doyle, but in 1897 the Royal Hotel was dethroned and the closed signs went up. Not a trace of the building remains today, although there is one small reminder that the Marquis of Done-'em-all once lived here. The gardens of the property were on the corner of Donegall Square and on this land now stands a seven-storey office block called Donegall House. No doubt the spendthrift marquis would have been wryly amused to discover that Donegall House is now the head-quarters of a bank.

SAM'S BAR | *16–18 Gaffikin Street*

Named after Samuel Hill, who owned this pub on the corner of Blondin Street from 1964 until its closure in the mid-1970s, Sam's Bar had been previously known as the Cosy Bar, but in truth it was the pub's nickname that made it memorable. It is said that the swing door leading into the bar had a striking depiction of a bare-breasted milkmaid and so this pub became known to its regulars as 'The Swingin' Diddy'.

The bar had a long history, stretching back to the latter years of the 19th century when it was owned by Margaret Black. She ran the place until 1919 when a Mr T. Agnew took over and remained the proprietor for 22 years. W. J. Croskery succeeded Agnew in 1941, and other owners between then and 1964 included William Brown and Harold Irwin. By 1977, however, the Swingin' Diddy swung no more and Sam's Bar was just a vacant piece of ground.

THE SPANISH ROOMS | *41 Divis Street*

Known to its regulars as the 'Cider House' or the 'Scrump House', this popular entertainment spot, which played host to big names in the Sixties like Roger Whittaker and Joe Dolan, was even more famous for its range of ciders. And not just the rough house stuff, but quality handmade brews from cider makers large and small. Some of the more potent offerings even came in small shot glasses.

Most of it, however, must have been served in much larger glasses, since it was reckoned in 1972 that customers were working their way through 900 gallons (or 7,200 pints) of cider every week. Some have estimated that as much as 65,000 gallons of cider went down the hatch annually during the heyday of the Spanish Rooms, making it the biggest seller of cider in the British Isles.

Besides the attraction of his cider range, owner James Coyle had two notable exhibits in the bar – a one million dollar bill issued by the Confederate States of America and one of the first ever £1 notes to be issued by the Bank of Ireland in 1813.

There was a pub on this site for many years, stretching back to Samuel Weir's spirit grocers in the 1870s, but the heyday of the Spanish Rooms was a comparatively short, if memorable, six or seven years in the 1960s and early 1970s. When the premises closed down the building lay derelict for some time before finally being demolished. Cider manufacturers everywhere must have been mightily upset.

THE SPORTSMANS' ARMS | *313 York Street*

This dockland bar was founded in the 1920s on the corner of Ship Street and was initially owned by the Madden Brothers, who at the time were also the proprietors of THE MORNING STAR in Pottinger's Entry, the Dufferin House in nearby Whitla Street and the Ivy Bar in Church Lane. W. J. McQuillan took over the premises in the early 1950s and in its final years in the 1960s and 1970s the pub was owned by Barney Conway. In his book, *Memories of York Street*, dockland writer John Campbell said of Conway: 'He gave us tick and never pressed for payment. He also provided monies to put over some weddings, and many a pram trundling up and down York Street was paid for by cash borrowed from him'. The Sportsmans' Arms was demolished in the late 1960s or early 1970s and was a vacant site by 1972. 'On the night it fell,' recalls Campbell, 'the drink flowed and it was free, courtesy of Barney'.

THE STAG'S HEAD | *Rosemary Street*

It is thought that this site on the corner of Rosemary Street and North Street was occupied by a pub from the early 1700s. Little is known about it, however, until the beginning of the 1800s, when Dan Miskelly ran a coaching inn and undertakers under the name of the Buck's Head. The coaches connected the inn with Derry/Londonderry and destinations in north Antrim. Sometime around 1839 the inn was renamed The Stag's Head and the exterior was decorated with a pair of antlers. The inn remained in existence at least until 1890 and possibly as late as 1910.

THE STAR AND GARTER | *47–49 Rosemary Street*

A long-established tavern whose chief claim to fame was the story that it had a secret tunnel connecting it with the house of Belfast's Provost Marshal in High Street. The supposed tunnel was featured in *The Green Cockade*, one of a series of popular novels about the 1798 Rising written by Margaret T. Pender, whose long and prolific literary career lasted from 1884 until her death on St Patrick's Day in 1920.

The bar was still serving customers and still known as the Star and Garter in the mid-1970s, almost 200 years after the 1798 Rising. At the beginning of the 20th century the tavern was owned by John Byrne, who was also the licensee of the Princess Bar a couple of doors away. When Francis Bradley took over The Star and Garter in 1922 it had been amalgamated with The Princess Bar and later, when John Bradley was in charge, the pub occupied premises at both 43–45 and 47–49 Rosemary Street. Between them was the stockbroking business of W. J. Richardson, which had been there since before the end of the 19th century.

Last orders were called for The Star and Garter around 1977, although what happened to the secret tunnel – if indeed it ever existed – remains a mystery.

THE STORE BAR | *21 Church Lane*

Built in 1905 on the site of the former premises of Magill and Cinnamond, wine and tea merchants, this tidy little bar with its small snugs, cut glass mirrors, carved

The striking façade of The Store Bar in the 1930s
(Hogg Collection, Ulster Museum)

wooden bar and curving windows is perhaps best known because of its founder. He was Alexander McCann, of the famous Belfast pub-owning family whose Braithwaite and McCann partnership owned a chain of pubs throughout the city for many years (see HATFIELD HOUSE). Not only was the Store one of the chain's flagship bars, it also served for many years as the head office of A. McCann Ltd – the firm which succeeded Braithwaite and McCann.

Alexander lived past the age of 100 and his photograph took pride of place in the Store Bar. A wood-panelled lounge was created upstairs and there was also a restaurant called the Causerie where roast duck would have set you back 11 shillings and sixpence in 1972. Some years afterwards, the Store Bar, the cosy little snugs and the 11-bob duck were swallowed up by redevelopment.

THE THEATRE TAVERN and THE SHAKESPEARE HOTEL

19 and 21
Castle Lane

It is hardly surprising to learn that The Theatre Tavern and The Shakespeare Hotel, two adjoining premises at the Arthur Square end of Castle Lane, were the frequent haunts of actors and music hall performers in the latter half of the 19th century. The proprietor of the Theatre Tavern was 'Ould Bob' Donnelly, famous for his luxuriant whiskers and his encyclopedic knowledge of the theatre. The bar itself had windows etched with scenes from *Hamlet* and *Othello*.

'Ould Bob' gave up the tavern in the early 1860s, and its name was changed to the Ulster Bar by the new owners, the Murtagh family. They continued to run the place until the mid-1890s when it was snapped up by the Bodega Company.

The Shakespeare Hotel, meanwhile, wasn't content to be a mere watering hole for performers – it ended up providing a stage for them. The hotel was next door to the residence of the manager of the Theatre Royal in Arthur Street and was initially run by Tom Frazer, then by D. McNab. From 1852 until the late 1870s, the hotel's concert room was developed into the Shakespeare Music Hall under the guidance of Edward Prior Grey and his daughter. Historian Alfred S. Moore described the Shakespeare's music saloon as 'the pioneer of modern variety theatre'.

THE ULSTER TAVERN | *89 Chichester Street*

The proximity of this mock Tudor bar to the city's Royal Courts of Justice was both its lifeblood and its downfall. Situated on the corner of Lower Chichester Street and Victoria Street, the snugs of this traditional old pub would resound every lunchtime to the gossip of the legal profession as barristers, clerks, solicitors and their clients jostled for service at the high counter. But in July 1985, it was a terrorist bomb aimed at the courthouses where many of the tavern's customers worked that put paid to their favourite after-hours watering hole.

Despite appearances, the Ulster Tavern was not a particularly old pub. It was built around 1920 to a design by W. J. Moore, who was also the architect of a number of private houses on the Malone Road, and was the second bar to be

The Ulster Tavern in c.1930 – the bar was a popular haunt for legal professionals and their clients
(Hogg Collection, Ulster Museum)

located on that site. Part of the Braithwaite and McCann chain of pubs, it also featured a busy restaurant called the Tavern Buttery, which a 1967 eating-out guide called 'one of the best places in Belfast in which to have a meal or drink'.

THE WASHINGTON HOTEL | *15-21 Howard Street*

George Washington, the first President of the United States, is claimed to be descended from folk who once lived at Mount Vernon, in the Fortwilliam area of north Belfast, and it's generally accepted that this supposed connection was the inspiration for the naming of The Washington Hotel. However, George Washington died in 1799 and it was perhaps another 60 years or so before the name of The Washington Hotel became well known. Around 1870 there was also a Belfast spirit merchant named George Washington who had premises in Ann Street and it is possible that he may have had some connection with the business. The truth of it all is a little uncertain.

Certainly The Washington Hotel was a thriving business in 1870. It had a large clientele, mostly drawn from the professional classes and the theatre crowd, although even church folk were known to patronise the premises. In 1872, for example, the *Belfast Daily Times* reported that the Presbytery of Belfast was entertained to a sumptuous dinner by members of the congregation at The Washington Hotel.

Travellers also regularly frequented the Washington since it was the nearest watering hole to Belfast's first public transport system. A two-route service of horse trams operated until the end of the 19th century from a terminus at Wellington Street just behind the hotel, which at this time was run by a Benjamin L. Firth. One tram route ran to Botanic Gardens in the south of the city while the other took passengers to the Midland Hotel in York Street.

Over the years, the Washington gradually abandoned its hotel status and became generally known as the Washington Bar. In 1912 it was purchased by Thomas McGeough, a native of Ballybay, Co. Monaghan, for the sum of £4,500. The price included the purchase of an adjoining property into which the Washington promptly expanded. Under the astute management of Mr McGeough the bar continued to grow in popularity, and after his death in 1947, the premises were sold for a record price of £36,000.

Up until that time, the most expensive bar in Ireland had been Nagles in Talbot Street, Dublin, which had been sold for £33,000. An *Irish News* correspondent who witnessed the Washington sale was impressed by the enthusiastic bidding for the premises. 'Prospective buyers from all parts of Ireland were present and, from the first bid of £20,000 until the premises were eventually knocked down, there was spirited competition, £1,000 being added each time by a word or a slight nod of the head. The price is stated to be far above any paid for a public house in Ireland, but although the majority of those attending the sale were surprised there were also a few who expressed the opinion that the last two years was an indication that the price would be a record one.'

The record price the Washington commanded in 1947 was in marked contrast to the amount paid for the premises in 1961. In a private transaction the bar was sold to James Henry McAlinden for exactly the same price that had been paid for it 14 years earlier, £36,000. It wasn't that the business was declining – on the contrary, the Washington was more popular than ever – it was just that the potential list of big-spending buyers had shrunk. The owners had hoped to keep publicity about the disappointing price to a minimum, but a high-profile court action brought by estate agents involved in the sale let the cat out of the bag.

In the 1960s, a Belfast guidebook noted that the Washington 'was, and still is, a favourite rendezvous for the patrons of the cinemas in Great Victoria Street and Fisherwick Place and has a long connection with the theatrical and musical life of the city. Under the ownership of the present host, Mr Joe McAlinden, the large public bar has retained much of the character which made it what it was in former years.'

Affectionately known as 'The Wash', the premises were extensively refurbished in 1988 and the marble counter and snugs were replaced by contemporary tiling, wood and brass. In recent years, the bar has been restyled once again and renamed Shenanagan's.

THE WEE HOUSE | *Albert Street and Berlin Street*

The Wee House in Albert Street was a small corner pub which was famous at one time for its traditional music sessions. Crowds of people would squeeze into the tiny bar whenever a group of musicians gathered to perform. Children from the surrounding houses would be despatched to the Wee House to fetch a jug of porter as recently as the late 1950s. The Albert Street pub was just one of a number of Belfast bars to be given the name the Wee House, since many of them were small establishments situated on a street corner with a family living above the premises. There was another Wee House at the corner of Berlin Street and in the Shankill, which is believed to have survived up until the early 1980s. But it, like all the other Wee Houses in the city, has long since closed its doors for good.

THE WHEATFIELD BAR | *Crumlin Road*

It's hard to say now if these two facts are connected, but the Wheatfield was reckoned to be the venue for eight out of ten local wedding receptions in the 1960s and it was also at one time the biggest seller of Guinness porter in Ireland.

The bar takes its name from a time when pockets of arable land could still be found around the city. The rising ground approaching Ardoyne Retreat was known locally as the wheat field since it was used for planting crops until comparatively recent times. Now, of course, it has completely disappeared under encroaching development.

There was a bar on the site as far back as the First World War, and the finely detailed craftmanship of the early 1920s was still in evidence right up until the Wheatfield's untimely end in the early years of the Troubles. The popular pub's heyday was in the 1960s when it was owned by former Antrim Gaelic footballer Paddy O'Hara and was one of the busiest bars in the area.

THE WHEATSHEAF | *1 May Street*

In 1820, if you had told a friend that you would meet them for a drink in the Wheatsheaf, they might have ended up at any one of four locations across the city. For in addition to The Wheatsheaf in May Street, which was owned by Andrew Gibson, there was also a Wheatsheaf in Ann Street, owned by William Dunlop, another in North Street, owned by Mary Scott, and one in Ballyhackamore, owned by Robert Tomen.

The May Street tavern was particularly popular with country folk who visited the town on fair days. The street was named after the influential May family, who owned the nearby May's Fields, where a monthly fair was held, as well as May's Market and St George's Market. Purveyors of produce who came into the city from the country to sell their goods would often quench their thirst, have a bite to eat and sometimes strike a deal or two at The Wheatsheaf. The bar and its three namesakes are all long gone, the May Street tavern being replaced by a private dwelling in 1867 and later by Henry Matier and Co., linen handkerchief manufacturers, before making way for a modern six-storey office block.

THE WHITE CROSS INN | *Castle Place (and later North Street)*

The Belfast Harp Festival of 1792 heralded a revival of interest in Irish traditional music that chimed with the growing mood of radicalism and nationalism that was sweeping late 18th-century Belfast. The festival was arranged to coincide with the third anniversary of the storming of the Bastille and ten harpers took part, six of whom were blind, the youngest aged just 15 and the oldest 97. The festival was followed five years later by the publication of Edward Bunting's *Ancient Irish Music*, a transcription of airs he collected on his travels throughout Ireland, and on St Patrick's Day 1808 by the formation of the Belfast Harp Society.

The venue for the formation of the society was Lynn's Hotel, an establishment next door to the Donegall Arms Hotel and run by a man named Pat Lynn. The man selected as the society's first teacher was Arthur O'Neill, a blind harper from County Tyrone who was in his mid-70s at the time. The Belfast Harp Society survived a mere five years, however, before sinking due to lack of funds in 1813.

The name of Lynn's Hotel similarly disappeared, to be replaced by The White Cross Inn, which in 1819, under the ownership of Mary Graham, moved to a new location in North Street (a few doors away from what is now THE DEER'S HEAD pub). The inn remained at this location until the 1980s, when the site became derelict. In 1988 the White Cross licence was transferred to Frames Bar in Library Street and all traces of the inn were blotted out by redevelopment.

WHITE'S TAVERN | *2–4 Winecellar Entry*

The narrow lanes off High Street are home to some of Belfast's most historic pubs, and at one time Winecellar Entry was narrower than most. The former Bigart's Alley was just six feet wide and some say that if you had strolled down this tight passageway in the year 1630 you would have come across the forerunner of White's Tavern.

There are, however, differing theories about the origins of the bar. One version states that the premises were bought in 1630 by Thomas Kane who established a tavern there, but it has been claimed elsewhere that it was an English family called Bateson who founded a wine and spirit store, rather than a tavern, in Winecellar Entry in the late 1600s.

Certainly, the building appears to have been used as a spirit warehouse in the late 18th century, following extensive building work which was carried out by a wine merchant named Valentine Jones. Jones was by all accounts a colourful character. Married at 16, he lived to the remarkable age of 94, and on his 90th birthday he danced the night away at the city's Assembly Rooms in the company of his son, grandson and great-grandson, all of whom were also called Valentine Jones.

In 1803 the property passed into the hands of a James Napier and for a while it was owned by William Park and Company. Then in the 1850s a wholesale spirit merchant called Hugh White assumed ownership of the building, giving it the name it carries today. White was a remarkably progressive businessman who was quick to see the advantage of new technology. As early as 1899 he had installed a telephone at his Winecellar Entry premises – the number was Belfast 526 – and he also had a telegraph address, 'Butts', inspired by the name given to wine casks.

Although the evidence suggests that it may not always have been a public house, there seems little doubt that White's Tavern has links with the drinks trade stretching back over four centuries – except perhaps for a brief period in the 1870s when 2 Winecellar Entry was the Belfast Arms Temperance Hotel and any kind of strong drink would have been frowned upon by its owners.

No such restrictions apply at White's Tavern today, however. Following an extensive programme of restoration work carried out in the 1980s, the style of both the exterior and the interior is designed to reflect the rich heritage of one of Belfast's oldest drinks emporiums.

Above: tilework detail from the façade of Hatfield House

Index

Bibliography

Adams, Gerry, *Before the Dawn*, Heinemann, London, 1996

Bardon, Jonathan, *Belfast*, The Blackstaff Press, Belfast, 1983

Bardon, Jonathan, *A History of Ulster*, The Blackstaff Press, Belfast, 1992

Barton, Brian, *The Blitz: Belfast in the War Years*, The Blackstaff Press, Belfast, 1989

Beckett, J.C. et al, *Belfast: The Making of a City*, Appletree Press, Belfast, 1988

The Best Places To Eat and Drink in Northern Ireland, The City Directory Company, 1967

Brett, C.E.B., *Buildings of Belfast*, Friar's Bush Press, Belfast, 1985

Bulson, Roy, *Ulster Inns and Taverns*, Northern Whig, Belfast, 1972

Campbell, John, *Memories of York Street*, North Belfast History Workshop, Belfast, 1991

Keyes, John (editor), *Sam Thompson: Over the Bridge and Other Plays*, Lagan Press, Belfast, 1997

Killen, John (editor), *The Decade of the United Irishmen*, The Blackstaff Press, Belfast, 1997

Kirk, Bill, *The Klondyke Bar*, The Blackstaff Press, Belfast, 1975

Larmour, Paul, *The Architectural Heritage of Malone and Stranmillis*, Ulster Architectural Heritage Society, Belfast, 1991

Maguire, W.A., *Belfast*, Keele University Press, Keele, 1993

McCann, Donna, *The Row You Know: Memories of Old Sandy Row*, Sandy Row Community Centre Committee, Belfast, 1997

Moore, Alfred S., *Old Belfast*, Carter Publications, 1951

Newmann, Kate, *Dictionary of Ulster Biography*, Institute of Irish Studies, Belfast, 1993

O'Byrne, Cathal, *As I Roved Out*, The Blackstaff Press, Belfast, 1982 – first published by the Irish News Ltd, 1946

Patton, Marcus, *Central Belfast: A Historical Gazetteer*, Ulster Architectural Heritage Society, Belfast, 1993

Pollock, Vivienne and Parkhill, Trevor, *Belfast: Old Photographs*, Sutton Publishing Ltd, Sutton, 1997

Tohill, J.J., *Pubs of the North*, (not published) 1990

Wallace, Martin, *100 Irish Lives*, David and Charles, London, 1993

Wine and Dine in Northern Ireland, Technical Sales Promotions, Belfast, 1970

Acknowledgements

Thanks are due to the following people for their kind assistance and encouragement in the compilation of this book: Judy Crawford, Anne Diver and staff of the Federation of the Retail Licensed Trade NI, Joe Graham, Keith Haines, Alan Irvine and the patrons of the Great Eastern Bar, John Killen and the staff of the Linen Hall Library, Seamas mag-Fhionnghaile, Frank O'Neill, Belfast Central Library and Newspaper Library, and the Public Record Office of Northern Ireland.

Photographic credits:
© Appletree Press: pp 3, 17, 46, 89 & cover (Hatfield House tiles; The Beehive); © Belfast City Council: pp 6, 18, 20, 27, 34, 50, 52, 60, 62, 66, 74 & cover (Robinson's clock; bar cabinet, The Blackthorn; window, The Morning Star; Bittle's Bar; barrels, White's Tavern; tiles, Crown Liquor Saloon); © Belfast Telegraph Newspapers Ltd: pp 28, 41 & 48; Courtesy of Botanic Inns Ltd: pp 22, 38, 68 & 78; Courtesy of Joe Graham: p 56; Courtesy of Frank O'Neill: p 76; Photographs reproduced with the kind permission of the Trustees of the National Museums and Galleries of Northern Ireland: pp 15, 37, 43, 65, 80, 83 & 85.

Notes